Life Changing Journey

500 Inspirational Quotes

SERIES VI

"Unveiling Wisdom: Inspiring Quotes to Spark Your Life. A Treasury of Inspiration for Cultivating Positivity on Life, Love, Nature, and More."

SHREE SHAMBAV

Life Changing Journey
Inspirational Quotes - Series – VI
Shree Shambav

Published by Shree Shambav, Tamil Nadu, India
Shree Shambav Ink & Imagination "Where Words Breathe and Imagination Soars"

First Edition, 2025

ISBN: 978-93-342-8218-4
Email: shreeshambav@gmail.com
Web: www.shambav.org

DEDICATION

"Isavasyam idam sarvam yat kim ca jagatyam jagat, tena tyaktena bhunjitha, ma gridhah kasyasvid dhanam"

To the Almighty,

the Divine Masters,

the family who listens,

and my parents who see –

your presence shapes the pages of my life's journey.

"Isavasyam idam sarvam yat kim ca jagatyam jagat"

Meaning: "God encompasses everything you perceive, see, or touch with your sense organs."

DISCLAIMER

This book, *"Life-Changing Journey - Inspirational Quotes: Series VI,"* is a heartfelt compilation of personal reflections and insights born from the author's journey of understanding life and the natural world. Each inspirational quote is a subjective truth—a distillation of experience and thought—meant to serve as a mirror for readers to explore their own perspectives and uncover meaning through the lens of their unique experiences.

The intention behind this book is to share a message imbued with compassion, love, and care. It is designed to inspire readers on their personal journeys and guide them toward discovering the deeper realities of life. This is not a prescriptive manual but an invitation to pause, reflect, and engage with life's profound yet simple truths.

It's important to acknowledge that neither the content nor the sequence of the quotes is intended to cause harm, discomfort, or conflict with the reader's personal beliefs. Should any part of the book feel unsettling or contradictory to one's convictions, it is purely coincidental and never intentional.

The journey through these quotes is one of openness and fluidity, free from rigid interpretations or dogmatic assertions. The content reflects the author's personal perspective, humbly offered as a source of inspiration and gentle guidance. Readers are invited to engage with the material at their own pace, to reflect deeply, and to adapt the wisdom within to align with their inner truths and life experiences.

Above all, this book aspires to spark joy, nurture connection, and encourage purposeful living. It gently beckons readers to cultivate a life rooted in compassion, integrity, and intentionality, while embracing the beauty of each moment with grace and mindfulness. May the words within these pages illuminate your path as you embark on a transformative journey of self-discovery, growth, and renewal. The journey is uniquely yours, and it is an honour for the author to accompany you, even if only in spirit, as you navigate the unfolding of your life.

With this understanding, readers are encouraged to approach the book with an open mind and heart, recognising that its wisdom is offered not as universal truth but as a collection of insights shaped by the author's personal experiences. You are invited to absorb what resonates, reinterpret what feels unfamiliar, and find your own meaning within these words.

Ultimately, the author's deepest wish is that these reflections serve as a beacon of hope, a source of motivation, and a catalyst for positivity as you embark on your life-changing journey. May this book inspire you to walk your path with courage, grace, and an unwavering belief in the beauty of life's unfolding.

Note - If any part of the book, in any sequence, hurts the reader's sentiments, it would be just out of a sheer accident, not intentional

Divine

"In the tender embrace of surrender lies a profound revelation—the raw, unspoken beauty of union. Each ripple of the river becomes a whispered confession, a declaration of belonging to something greater than itself. As the river flows ceaselessly, unveiling its eternal unity with the boundless ocean, so too does the soul, in its sacred act of surrender, unveil its timeless connection to the Divine.

This surrender is not a loss but a metamorphosis of unparalleled grace, where the fragmented self dissolves into the infinite. And in that dissolution, the soul discovers the ineffable depth of its true essence—a profound oneness with the Divine, unbroken and eternal. It is a sacred symphony, an eternal melody that reverberates through the very fabric of existence, calling us back to the home we never truly left."

– Shree Shambav

EPIGRAM

"In silence, we remember. In struggle, we awaken.
In the whispers of life, truth finds its voice."

– Shree Shambav

Life Changing Journey

500 Inspirational Quotes

Shree Shambav

Shree Shambav is a 29x best-selling author renowned for his transformative works in personal development and spiritual growth.

Dear Cherished Readers

Dear Cherished Readers,

As I embark on this new literary voyage, my heart swells with profound gratitude and an overwhelming sense of connection. With deep emotion, I extend my heartfelt appreciation to each of you who has joined me on this journey.

With sincere warmth, I invite you to revisit the steps we have taken together through the pages of my earlier works. Our odyssey began with "Journey of Soul - Karma," a book that marked my first foray into the world of words and a testament to the raw passion that ignited my writing adventure.

The subsequent chapters of our shared narrative unfolded through the enchanting tapestry of the "Twenty + One" series. Each page turned was a brushstroke on the canvas of our imaginations, painting vivid stories that I hoped would resonate deeply within your hearts.

And how can I forget the transformative journey we embarked on with the "Life Changing Journey -

Inspirational Quotes Series." Day by day, quote by quote, we delved into reflections that uplifted, inspired, and sought to bring a glimpse of light to our souls.

The release of "Death - Light of Life and the Shadow of Death" promises to shed new light on the timeless mystery of death. Similarly, "Unleashing the Incredible Potential of Programming with Python - Optimum - PYTHON: Ultimate Guide for Beginners Series I" is poised to empower readers with newfound knowledge.

In addition, my technical book, OPTIMUM Python Series II - Exploring Data Structures and Algorithms, delves into advanced concepts in Python programming, offering a comprehensive guide for those seeking to deepen their understanding.

Shree Shambav expands his artistic repertoire with "*Whispers of Eternity: 150 Plus - A Symphony of Soulful Verses*," a heartfelt exploration of the human experience. Alongside this, his "*Whispers of the Soul: A Journey Through Haiku*" distils profound insights into poignant verses. Together, these works showcase his versatility and mastery of soulful expression, inviting readers on a journey of self-discovery. Through his poetry, he weaves a rich tapestry of emotion that resonates deeply with the heart.

Shree Shambav's latest works—*Learn to Love Yourself: A Journey of Discovering Inner Beauty and Strength Through 10 Transformative Rules, The Power of Letting Go: Embrace Freedom and Happiness, A Journey of Lasting Peace—are true treasures of self-discovery, The Entitlement Trap: Get Over It, Get On, Whispers of a Dying Soul: Unspoken Regrets and Unlived Dreams, Whispers of Silence - Unlocking Inner Power through Stillness, The Power of Words: Transforming Speech, Transforming Lives, The Art of Intentional Living: Minimalism for a Life of Purpose, Awakening the Infinite:The Power of Consciousness in Transforming Life, Beyond the Veil: A Journey Through Life After Death series, Bonds Beyond Blood - Where love builds bridges, and bonds defy blood., and A Journey into Spiritual Maturity - 12 Golden Rules for Inner Transformation.*

In addition to these works, Shree Shambav has recently ventured into astrology with the release of Astrology Unveiled – Foundations of Ancient Wisdom Series I to VIII, expanding into the realm of metaphysics. These books explore the foundational principles of Vedic astrology, offering readers a rich and practical understanding of this ancient wisdom.

Your unwavering support, enthusiasm to immerse yourself in my writings, and readiness to embark on these journeys with me have been my greatest sources of inspiration. Your input has been a beacon guiding me through the creation process, moulding these stories into containers of passion, emotion, knowledge, and resonance.

As I unveil this new narrative before you, know that your presence, insights, and shared moments have been my companions. The path we have walked together is etched in the annals of my creative evolution, and it's an honour beyond words to have you by my side once more.

Here's to the readers who have illuminated my path with their presence, who have embraced my stories with open hearts, and who have woven themselves into the very fabric of my literary world. Our journey has been a symbiotic dance of writer and reader, a harmony of souls brought together by the magic of storytelling.

With a heart brimming with appreciation and eyes glistening with anticipation, I extend my deepest gratitude for your unwavering support. Thank you for the memories, the shared emotions, and the countless hours spent in the worlds we've crafted together. As we step into this new adventure, let's continue to explore, feel, and discover the boundless horizons that words can unveil.

Warmly,

Shree Shambav

Suggested Reads

FROM BEST-SELLING AUTHOR

Endorsements

"In a world that moves too fast and speaks too loud, this book is a gentle invitation to pause, breathe, and listen to the quiet truths within. With poetic grace and soul-stirring wisdom, Shree Shambav offers more than words—he offers a mirror, a sanctuary, and a companion for the inner journey. Every page holds a light for those walking through uncertainty and a deeper resonance for those seeking meaning, healing, and self-discovery. This is not just a book; it is a sacred conversation between the soul and the infinite."

- Manju Reshma (Educationalist)

About the Author

Shree Shambav is an internationally acclaimed, best-selling author, inspirational speaker, artist, philanthropist, life coach, and entrepreneur. A world record holder, his deep passion for music led him to create soul-stirring albums, drawing inspiration from his celebrated poetry collection, Whispers of Eternity. His profound insights have sparked deep personal transformations, guiding countless individuals toward self-discovery, purposeful living, and authenticity.

With an extraordinary ability to unlock human potential, Shree empowers individuals to break through limitations and embrace their highest selves. His writings, lectures, and compassionate guidance continue to uplift lives, fostering resilience, mindfulness, and personal growth.

Shree Shambav is a 29x best-selling author celebrated for his profound contributions to personal development and spiritual growth.

Shree Shambav's literary journey took flight with the celebrated Journey of Soul - Karma, where he delved into the depths of human experience to unveil profound insights. Garnering recognition through multiple literature awards, his repertoire includes esteemed works, such as the Twenty + One Series and the enlightening Life Changing Journey series.

As a distinguished alumnus of the Indian Institute of Management and the National Institute of Technology, Shree Shambav brings a wealth of corporate acumen from his tenure in multinational corporations. His most recent publications, including Unveiling the Enigma, Death - Light of Life and the Shadow of Death and Optimum - Python Series I and Series II, demonstrate his mastery of both the literary and technical spheres.

Shree Shambav expands his artistic repertoire with "*Whispers of Eternity: 150 Plus - A Symphony of Soulful Verses,*" a heartfelt exploration of the human experience. Alongside this, his "*Whispers of the Soul: A Journey Through Haiku*" distils profound insights into poignant verses. Together, these works showcase his versatility and mastery of soulful expression, inviting readers on a journey of self-discovery. Through his poetry, he weaves a rich tapestry of emotion that resonates deeply with the heart.

Shree Shambav's latest works—*Learn to Love Yourself: A Journey of Discovering Inner Beauty and Strength Through 10 Transformative Rules, The Power of Letting Go: Embrace Freedom and Happiness, A Journey of Lasting Peace—are true treasures of self-discovery, The Entitlement Trap: Get Over It, Get On, Whispers of a Dying Soul: Unspoken Regrets and Unlived Dreams, Whispers of Silence - Unlocking Inner Power through Stillness, The Power of Words: Transforming Speech, Transforming Lives, The Art of Intentional Living: Minimalism for a Life of Purpose, Awakening the Infinite:The Power of Consciousness in Transforming Life, Beyond the Veil: A Journey Through Life After Death series, Bonds Beyond Blood - Where love builds bridges, and bonds defy blood., and A Journey into Spiritual Maturity - 12 Golden Rules for Inner Transformation.*

In addition to these works, Shree Shambav has recently ventured into astrology with the release of Astrology Unveiled – Foundations of Ancient Wisdom Series I to VIII, expanding into the realm of metaphysics. These books explore the foundational principles of Vedic astrology, offering readers a rich and practical understanding of this ancient wisdom.

Shree Shambav established the Ayur Rakshita Foundation, which is dedicated to promoting boundless growth, universal fraternity, and environmental protection. The charity helps diverse communities while working for societal progress.

To learn more about Shree Shambav and his works, visit his website at www.shambav.org. For information about the Ayur Rakshita Foundation and its initiatives, visit www.shambav-ayurrakshita.org.

Let's Follow him on Social Media: **@shreeshambav**

PREFACE

Life is a symphony, where each moment plays a unique note in the grand composition of existence. Within this melody, words possess a timeless power—they awaken, heal, and inspire. *'Life Changing Journey - Inspirational Quotes Series"* by Shree Shambav is not just a collection of phrases; it is a companion, a guide, and a beacon for those navigating the intricate pathways of life.

This book was conceived in the quiet spaces where inspiration is born—in those still moments when the noise of the world fades and the soul begins to speak. Every quote in this collection distils universal truths into simple yet profound expressions, echoing the essence of human experience. Through these pages, you are invited to embark on a journey of self-discovery, reflection, and transformation.

The chapters are thoughtfully crafted, each offering a thematic exploration of the human spirit. They illuminate the courage required to embrace change, the resilience to chase dreams, and the wisdom to find meaning amid life's adversities. They delve into love and relationships, the beauty of self-acceptance, and the quiet strength that lies dormant within. These chapters whisper of joy found in simplicity, gratitude awakened through mindfulness, and the profound connection we share with the natural world and the cosmos.

This book is a tapestry woven with timeless insights that transcend circumstances. It invites you to pause, reflect, and draw inspiration from the wellspring of human wisdom. Whether you are weathering life's storms, seeking the motivation to pursue your aspirations, or yearning for the serenity of inner peace, these quotes serve as a trusted guide and confidant.

In Series III, themes like *"Embracing Change," "Discovering Self," "Dreams and Aspirations," "Embracing Imperfections," "Finding Inner Strength,"* and *"Gratitude and Mindfulness"* invite you to reflect on identity, purpose, and the pursuit of your passions.

Series IV delves deeper into *"Inspiration and Motivation," "Lessons from Adversity," "Love and Relationships," "Nature's Symphony," "Pursuing Your Dreams,"* and *"Serenity and Balance"*—nurturing connections, fostering resilience, and celebrating life's harmony.

Series V culminates in the profound, with themes like *"Shades of Existence," "Success and Achievement," "The*

Beauty of Simplicity," "The Power of Kindness," and *"Wisdom from the Ages."* These chapters remind us to cherish the beauty in life's simplest moments and draw strength from timeless truths.

Series VI culminates in a journey of inner stillness and soulful reflection, exploring themes such as "Embracing Change," "Love and Relationships," "Serenity and Balance," "Shades of Existence," and "Whispers of the Divine." Each chapter gently invites us to slow down, to find meaning in silence, and to recognise the sacred in everyday life. They are reminders that life's simplest moments often carry the most profound truths and that true strength arises when we listen deeply—to others, to nature, and our own hearts.

Series VII deepens this introspection, guiding us through themes like "Discovering the Self," "Dreams and Aspirations," "Lessons from Adversity," "The Power of Kindness," and "Wisdom from the Ages." These chapters serve as lanterns on the path of growth—illuminating how hardship refines us, how kindness transforms, and how the wisdom of those who walked before us still echoes with relevance today. They remind us that every challenge holds a lesson, and every moment offers a choice to awaken.

Shree Shambav's words transcend the mundane, touching the sacred essence of life. They serve as gentle reminders of our shared humanity, encouraging us to embrace imperfections and live authentically. Each quote is a spark—a catalyst for growth and self-discovery, illuminating the path through life's trials and triumphs.

As you turn these pages, may you find not just words but a profound connection to your inner self and the world around you. Let this collection be a sanctuary of wisdom, a reservoir of courage, and a wellspring of inspiration, empowering you to embrace life with an open heart and an awakened soul.

Welcome to the *"Life Changing Journey - Inspirational Quotes Series."* May this book inspire you to live boldly, love deeply, and discover the boundless joy within your own journey.

Let the journey unfold.

With gratitude and encouragement,

Shree Shambav

INTRODUCTION

In a world that often feels like a whirlwind of expectations, responsibilities, and endless noise, it's easy to lose sight of the deeper meaning of life. We rush through our days, chasing goals and ticking off to-do lists, yet many of us long for something more—something that grounds us, inspires us, and reconnects us to the beauty of existence.

This longing is the seed from which the *"Life Changing Journey - Inspirational Quotes Series"* was born. At its heart, this book is an invitation—a gentle call to pause, reflect, and rediscover the wisdom that lies within and around us.

Words have an extraordinary ability to shape our perspectives and transform our lives. A single phrase encountered at the right moment, can shift our understanding, provide clarity in times of confusion, or ignite a spark of courage in the face of fear. This collection of quotes was curated with this transformative power in mind. Each one is a distillation of universal truths designed to speak directly to the soul and awaken the resilience, hope, and strength that reside within us all.

This book unfolds as a journey through a series of reflections, each thoughtfully curated to illuminate the many dimensions of the human experience.

Series VI reaches its culmination in profound contemplation, exploring themes such as "Embracing Change," "Love and Relationships," "Serenity and Balance," "Shades of Existence," and "Whispers of the Divine." These chapters serve as gentle companions, reminding us to honor the quiet power of transformation, to nurture meaningful connections, and to find beauty in the stillness of ordinary moments. They invite us to draw strength from the timeless truths that lie beneath the surface of everyday life—and to listen for the subtle, sacred whispers that guide us home to ourselves.

Through these reflections, you will uncover the resilience to navigate life's transitions, the courage to embrace your authentic self, and the joy of living with gratitude. Each theme is a stepping stone, leading you closer to understanding the beauty of imperfection and the strength that lies within.

As you journey through these pages, you will traverse a rich tapestry of themes that reflect the multifaceted nature of life. From the courage required to embrace change to the wisdom found in adversity, the tenderness of nurturing love and relationships, and the quiet strength discovered in gratitude and simplicity—each chapter serves as a portal to deeper self-reflection and understanding.

This series is not just a collection of words but a companion for your personal growth, offering profound insights that encourage you to live authentically and harmoniously.

But this book is not meant to be read in a rush. It is not a novel to be consumed from cover to cover in one sitting. Instead, it is a companion for life's journey, offering guidance and solace whenever you need it most. You might find comfort in a quote during a moment of despair, draw courage from a phrase when facing a challenge, or uncover a fresh perspective as you navigate a crossroads.

The beauty of this collection lies in its timelessness. Whether you're at the beginning of your journey, in the midst of transformation, or reflecting on lessons learned, these quotes will meet you where you are. They are not answers but mirrors, reflecting the wisdom you already possess and encouraging you to trust your inner voice.

We live in a time where the external world demands so much of us, yet the most profound answers often come from within. This book is a reminder to listen to that quiet voice—the one that whispers truths when the world falls silent. It is a guide to help you realign with your authentic self, find purpose amidst uncertainty, and celebrate the beauty of being alive.

As you turn the pages of this book, my hope is that you discover not just inspiration but a renewed sense of connection—to yourself, to others, and to the world around you. Let these quotes be your compass, pointing you toward a life of greater meaning, joy, and fulfilment.

This journey is yours to take. With each quote, may you find the courage to embrace your unique path and the wisdom to live it fully.

Welcome to the *"Life Changing Journey - Inspirational Quotes Series."* May these words guide you toward the light within and inspire you to create a life that resonates with your truest self.

With love and gratitude,

Warm regards,

Shree Shambav

PROLOGUE

In the hush of a still moment—when the noise of the world softens, when the demands of life momentarily pause—something extraordinary happens. The towering milestones we conquer do not measure a quiet truth that stirs within us, *but by the whispers of wisdom we gather in the shadows between them.*

These whispers rarely arrive with grandeur. They come softly—cloaked in joy, heartbreak, resilience, and surrender. They rise from quiet tears in the dark, from laughter shared under a setting sun, from the ache of letting go and the courage of beginning again. Each experience becomes a sacred messenger, delivering insight not just to the mind, but to the very soul.

This book is a collection of such whispers.

It is not a manual for success, nor a doctrine for living—it is a constellation of truths, tenderly stitched together from the fragments of human experience. Each quote is a flicker of light—subtle, but enduring. It does not tell you where to go, but it may help you see the path beneath your feet a little more clearly.

The inspiration for this work was not born in a single lightning flash, but in the slow burn of life itself. During sleepless nights wrapped in silence, amid nature's quiet symphonies, and in the fragile aftermath of both joy and sorrow, these words emerged—uninvited, yet deeply welcome. As though the universe, in its infinite compassion, was whispering back.

Because life is not a straight road. It's a mosaic—intricately woven with threads of uncertainty, transformation, and grace. Every trial, every triumph, every silent in-between moment adds colour and texture to the evolving story of who we are.

This book is an invitation to pause. To breathe. To listen—not just to the world outside but to the soft voice within. It is for the dreamers who reach beyond the sky, for the seekers who walk with questions, and for the wanderers who quietly carry their longing like lanterns.

As you turn these pages, may you find pieces of your own story reflected here—your doubts and your hopes, your falls and your risings. These quotes are not tied to any one time, place, or person. They are timeless truths, born from our shared humanity. They remind us that even in our solitude, we are never truly alone.

This is a journey of remembering—of returning to the sacred space within yourself where courage, peace, and purpose reside. It is not just about finding answers but about awakening the strength to live the questions fully, lovingly, and without fear.

May this book be your quiet companion. A flame in the dark. A pause when you are overwhelmed. A breath when you have forgotten how to breathe.

Welcome to the **"Life-Changing Journey – Inspirational Quotes Series."** This is not merely a book—it is a gentle guide, a soul offering, and a mirror reflecting the beauty, depth, and divine strength already within you.

With reverence and love,

Shree Shambav

CONTENTS

Embracing Change

Navigating Life's Transformations

"True transformation often begins with loss—the letting go of what we once clung to. From the ashes of old identities, a brighter, truer light emerges."

- *Shree Shambav*

Beyond the Shadows of Struggle

The inner battlefield is not a place of despair but of possibility—where every struggle is an invitation to rise beyond the shadows of the self.

Destiny's Whisper

"Fate does not shout—it whispers. Only those who are still enough to listen will hear where they are meant to go."

Love That Liberates

"True love does not ask you to choose between yourself and another. It walks beside you, not ahead or behind. It does not bind—it sets you free."

Love and the Fear of Losing Oneself

"True love does not ask you to surrender who you are, but it dares you to become more than you ever thought possible."

Rise from the Ashes

"You are not defined by the storms that break you, but by the fire within you that refuses to be extinguished."

Symphony of Suffering

"In the symphony of suffering, the pain you feel is not discordant notes but poignant messengers. Listen with all your heart, for within their melody lies the wisdom that leads to healing."

The Architect of Possibility

"In the vast landscape of life, uncertainty stands as the architect of possibility, constructing paths where none existed before."

The Art of Being

"The world teaches us to wear masks, but the soul longs to be bare."

The Art of Falling

"A leaf does not mourn the branch it once clung to; it simply trusts the wind to take it where it is meant to go."

The Art of Letting Go

"True freedom lies not in what we possess, but in the courage to release what no longer serves our journey."

The Art of Letting Go

"What you cling to most tightly may not be what sustains you, but what keeps you from soaring."

The Art of Surrender

"True freedom comes when we stop trying to control the world around us and instead learn to trust the unfolding of our own journey."

The Beauty of Becoming

"Growth is not a linear path but a series of unfolding moments—each challenge a stepping stone, each victory a breath of life."

The Burden of the Past

"A sailor never truly stops sailing—if not across the sea, then through the waves of his own memories, searching for a shore that no longer exists."

The Chains We Cannot See

"A man bound by gold and influence is no freer than one bound by iron and chains. The difference is only in the weight he chooses to carry."

The Chains of Gold

"We spend our lives chasing gold, only to realise too late that the more we carry, the less free we become."

The Chains of Wealth

"A man who owns nothing and fears nothing walks freer than a king bound by his own crown."

The Cost of Ambition

"We climb the highest peaks believing we will touch the sky, only to find the air too thin to breathe. Not every summit is worth the ascent."

The Courage to Begin Again

"It is not the fear of falling that holds us back, but the fear of not being able to rise again—yet every fall teaches us how to soar higher than before."

The Courage to Love

"Love is not the absence of fear, but the courage to embrace vulnerability, knowing that in giving our heart, we risk its breaking."

The Dance of Impermanence

"Life's beauty lies not in permanence, but in its fleeting rhythm. Like a dancer's step, it is precious because it ends."

The Dance of Light and Shadow

"Within each of us lives a dance of light and shadow. True peace is not found in banishing darkness but in embracing it as part of the whole."

The Echo of Unfinished Love

"Some absences are louder than presence. I never lost my love to time—I lost her to the silence that stretched between us, the unanswered questions, the love left in limbo." –

The Echoes of Loss

"Love does not die when it is lost. It lingers in the spaces we once shared, whispering in the silence, waiting to be found again."

The Echoes of Silence

"In the quiet of our hearts, we find answers we didn't know we were seeking, truths whispered by the soul when the world finally grows silent."

The Eternal Flame

"Within you burns a flame that neither time nor sorrow can extinguish. Guard it not with walls, but with wisdom."

The Eyes That Truly See

"To be seen for what you have is to be noticed; to be seen for who you are is to be understood."

The Fire That Consumes

"Desires, like fire, do not subside by feeding them. The more we give in to greed, the stronger it burns, reducing our peace to ashes. True satisfaction is found not in accumulation, but in contentment."

The Fire in a Sailor's Heart

"The ocean does not break a sailor; it reveals him. It strips him of all but his will to return home."

The Flower's Secret

"A flower does not fear the wind, for it knows that even in the harshest storms, its roots grow stronger beneath the soil."

The Forgotten Roads of Destiny

"The paths we abandon in search of greatness often lead us back to what our hearts sought all along."

The Freedom of Letting Go

"True freedom lies not in the abundance of things, but in the release of our attachment to them. When we let go, we make room for what truly nourishes our soul."

The Gift of Compassion

"To see another's heart is to touch their spirit, but to feel another's pain as your own is to transform both hearts in a way words cannot."

The Grace of Letting Go

"Sometimes the most powerful thing we can do is let go—not as a sign of defeat, but as a courageous act of trusting life's greater plan."

The Home Within

"A palace without love is a prison; a hut filled with kindness is a kingdom."

The Illusion of Appearances

"A man draped in silk may still shiver in the cold, while a beggar wrapped in rags may carry the warmth of a thousand suns."

The Illusion of Arrival

"Happiness is not a destination, nor is sorrow a prison—both are mere travelers passing through the landscapes of our soul."

The Illusion of Power

"The more we seek to control, the more we become prisoners of our own desires. True power is not in holding, but in knowing when to let go."

The Illusion of Time

"We measure life in years, yet the soul moves by moments. A single second of truth can outweigh a lifetime of certainty."

The Illusion of Walls

"A man builds walls to shelter himself from the world, only to realise they have become his prison."

The Journey Without End

"There is no true ending, only another beginning waiting beyond the horizon. Keep walking, keep dreaming, and let the winds of change guide you home."

The Journey to Self

"The longest journey we will ever take is the one inward, where we confront the shadows and emerge into the light of our truest self."

The Language of the Wind

"The wind does not carry words, yet it speaks to the soul. Listen—not with your ears, but with your heart."

The Light Within

"Each sunrise is a reminder that no matter how dark the night, the light within you is powerful enough to shine through any storm."

The Light of Resilience

"True strength is not in how we stand unbroken, but in how we rise after falling, our cracks filled with the light of resilience."

The Lightness of Letting Go

"It is not the weight of what we own, but the lightness of what we let go that frees us to live with meaning and grace."

The Measure of a Home

"A house may stand on pillars of stone, but a home is built on the warmth of shared laughter and love."

The Mirage of Desire

"Pleasure, when chased without wisdom, is like drinking saltwater—each sip only deepens the thirst."

The Mirage of More

"Greed whispers that the next possession, the next achievement, the next conquest will bring fulfillment. But like a mirage in the desert, each time we reach it, the thirst remains, and the chase begins again."

The Mirage of Pleasure

"Pleasure is like water cupped in the hands—refreshing for a moment, but it always slips through the fingers. Purpose, however, is the river that never runs dry."

The Paradox of Control

"The more we seek to control life, the more it slips through our fingers. True mastery is in surrender, in trusting life enough to let it flow freely."

The Path of Acceptance

"True strength lies not in resisting the tides of life but in allowing them to carry you forward, trusting that each wave leads to a greater shore."

The Path of Authenticity"

"Success is not measured by what we gain, but by how deeply we live, how truly we love, and how boldly we walk the path of our own truth."

The Path to True Freedom

"To master one's desires is not to live in deprivation, but to walk unchained."

The Peace Found in Self-Acceptance

"When we welcome our flaws as companions on the path, we unlock the doors to compassion and growth. In this acceptance, we find a peace that no external validation could ever bestow."

The Power of Diversity and Inclusion

"In the embrace of diversity and inclusion lies a transformative force that transcends superficial boundaries, weaving a fabric of respect and belonging where every voice, regardless of background, resonates with the harmony of progress."

The Power of Presence

"Happiness is not something to chase; it is found in the moments we slow down, breathe deeply, and allow ourselves to simply be."

The Power of Presence

"Life is not waiting in tomorrow's promises or yesterday's regrets. It is here, in this moment, that all of existence converges—open, alive, and eternally present."

The Power of Self-Reflection

"In the quiet moments of self-reflection, we uncover the profound truth that loving ourselves is the first step towards loving others deeply and authentically."

The Price of Power

"A man may gather gold and command nations, but if he loses himself in the pursuit, he will find that power is the most expensive thing he ever owned."

The Price of Power

"A throne built on influence is fragile, but a kingdom built on trust will never fall."

The Price of Wisdom

"A fool seeks treasure in gold, the wise man in experience, but only the broken understand that wisdom is bought with pain."

The Quiet Strength of Ignorance

The enemies within do not seek to destroy us outright; they thrive in our ignorance, growing stronger when we look away from the truth of who we are.

The River of Intention

"Life flows with grace when every addition is met with thoughtful release, like a river free of debris."

The Silence Between the Notes

"Music is not just sound—it is the silence between the notes, the space where emotions breathe, where souls speak without words."

The Silence of Truth

"Truth is not found in the noise of answers but in the quiet of understanding."

The Silent Cost of Success

"A man may stand atop the highest mountain and call himself victorious, but if he looks around and finds no one beside him, what has he truly won?"

The Silent Lessons of Wounds

"The deepest wounds often leave no scars on the skin, but carve silent wisdom into the soul, shaping who we become in the shadows of pain."

The Silent Transformation

"In the stillness of our deepest pain, a quiet transformation takes place, turning our scars into stories of survival and grace."

The Solitude of Success

"To stand atop a mountain of gold and find yourself alone is the greatest poverty of all."

The Strength in Embracing Our Shadows

"True self-acceptance is not found in perfection, but in the courage to embrace both light and shadow within ourselves. Only then do we discover the quiet strength that has always been ours."

The Strength in Softness

"To love yourself is not arrogance; it is the quiet strength of a river that knows its path, flowing forward without apology."

The True Measure of a Life

"The true measure of a life well lived is not in what you take with you, but in what you leave behind for others to grow from."

The Truth Beyond Gold

"Fortunes fade, walls crumble, but the love we nurture and the lives we touch—these are the only treasures time cannot steal."

The Twin Faces of Life

"Joy and sorrow walk hand in hand; to know one is to embrace the other. Only those who welcome both truly understand life."

The Un-Becoming Journey

"Perhaps the journey is not about becoming anything new, but about shedding all the layers of what you are not. It is in the un-becoming of everything that doesn't truly define you, that you uncover the essence of who you were always meant to be."

The Vanishing Moment

"Twilight does not cling to the sky, nor does the night chase the sun. All things come and go, and therein lies their beauty."

The Wealth of the Soul

"A man may hoard gold and power, yet remain poor in spirit. But one who is rich in wisdom and kindness, even with empty hands, possesses a treasure no greed can steal."

The Weight of Destiny

"We chase what we believe is meant for us, only to realise that destiny has been leading us elsewhere all along. The treasure I sought was gold, but perhaps the true wealth lies in saving a life."

The Weight of Dreams

"A dream is not a whisper; it is a fire. It does not ask for permission to burn—it only waits for you to decide whether you will fear its heat or become its flame."

The Weight of Indecision

"Every choice you avoid is a weight you carry. Lighten your soul by trusting your inner compass."

The Weight of Possession

"To own too much is to carry the world on your shoulders, forgetting that you were born to walk lightly upon it."

The Weight of Possessions

"The more a man owns, the heavier his heart becomes—for true wealth is measured not by what we keep, but by what we give away."

The Weight of Unfinished Journeys

"A road half-traveled is a story left incomplete, a question left unanswered, a dream abandoned before it can find its wings."

The Weight of Wealth

"A man may own the riches of the world, but if his soul is empty, he remains the poorest among beggars."

The Weight of Wealth

"Gold may buy comfort, but it cannot buy peace. A heavy purse can never fill an empty heart."

The Weight of Yesterday

"Memories are echoes that call us back, but they are not chains meant to hold us still. Honor the past, but do not let it steal your future."

The Weight of an Unfinished Journey

"Some journeys are not measured by distance, but by the weight they place upon the soul. And the heaviest of all is the one that leads you away from yourself."

The Whisper of Change

"Change does not ask for permission; it arrives like the wind—sometimes a whisper, sometimes a storm. The only choice we have is whether to resist or to dance."

Threads of Resilience

"In the intricate tapestry of life, every thread of challenge weaves into a masterpiece of resilience; patience reveals the beauty of 'everything happens for good.'"

Time is Fleeting

"Time slips through our fingers like sand; the moments we choose to hold onto define our lives."

Transforming Challenges into Opportunities

"A weak mind perceives only hurdles in all situations. A balanced mind sees challenges as obstacles to conquer. A strong mind, however, transforms these challenges into golden opportunities."

Trust Your Gut

"When you ignore your intuition, you abandon your own compass. Trust it, for it always points to your true north."

Unchanging Reality

"Do not tremble at the spectres of what is not real, for they are but fleeting whispers in the wind. Hold fast to the unchanging reality that has always been and will forever endure, untouched by the passage of time."

Unfolding Narratives

"To grasp the essence of today's unfolding story, one must first delve into the pages of yesterday's intricate narrative, for therein lie the profound lessons that shape our present and guide our future."

Unity in Diversity

"Each soul is like a unique note in the vast symphony of existence. It is only in harmony with others that we create music that echoes through eternity."

Unveiling Your Authentic Self

"In the quiet, we find the rare space to disentangle our true selves from the noise of the world. Silence strips away the layers of expectation and fear, revealing the authentic voice within—the one that knows who we are and what we seek."

Vintage Bonds of Friendship

"Friendship, a vintage wine, matures with time, gaining richness and depth. The older we get, the more we realise the profound worth of a good friend—someone who colors our past, walks beside us in the present, and casts a comforting shadow on the canvases of our future."

Whispers of the Soul

"Embrace the tears that fall as poignant whispers of your soul, for within each drop, a profound dialogue unfolds, revealing the profound truths your heart longs to share."

Workshops of Resilience

"Relationships tested by difficulty are the workshops where patience is honed, tolerance is chiselled, and forgiveness is the masterpiece painted on the canvas of resilience."

Love and Relationships

Nurturing Connections

"In every relationship, we meet not just the other—but ourselves. Love reveals the parts we hide, heals the wounds we deny, and invites us to grow through the reflection of another's soul."

- *Shree Shambav*

A Child's Crossroads

"Sometimes, courage is not about standing tall but about standing alone, even when it means defying those you love."

A Choice Beyond Redemption

"Every soul walks a fine line between shadow and light, but it's the smallest of choices—a word, a step, a single moment—that determines which side will define us."

A Family's Unbroken Thread

"Love is not the absence of fear but the defiance of it, the quiet resolve to stand together even when the fabric of trust feels worn thin."

A Father's Confession

"I spent my life building a fortress for my family, only to realise it kept out the storms but also the light."

Artist of Your Life

"To truly love yourself is to become the artist of your own life, painting each day with self-compassion and celebrating every hue of your journey, no matter how small."

Beacon of Kindness

"In the divine creation of my mother, I see the answer to why the world needed more kindness, her love a beacon of hope in a chaotic world."

Blooming with Self-Esteem

"In the garden of life, every moment of self-recognition is a flower blooming with self-esteem. Celebrate each blossom because it represents your journey and the unique beauty of your soul."

Blossoming Self-Love

"Self-acceptance is the seed that blossoms into self-love. When you embrace your true self, you open the door to a deep, real, and steadfast love."

Bonds Beyond Blood

"Family is not defined by lineage but by the bridges built with love. Where pride falters, understanding stands strong, binding hearts tighter than shared ancestry."

Boundless Devotion Quote

"Her love knows no bounds, embracing me even when my own heart falters, filling every void with unwavering devotion."

Bridges of Understanding

"A bridge is built not from stone but from trust, from the courage to meet someone in the middle. It takes vulnerability to step onto it and strength to cross it."

Building the Future, Forgetting the Present

"In the rush to build a future, don't forget the hands that hold you in the present."

Cherish Now

"Gratitude, for the present moment, transforms ordinary experiences into extraordinary memories; cherish now to build a life filled with love."

Compassionate Self-Love

"Self-love is the courage to see yourself through the lens of compassion, to honor your scars as symbols of survival, and to recognise that you are worthy of every ounce of kindness you so freely give to others."

Cornerstone of Progress

"Self-love serves as the cornerstone for personal progress. We develop a fulfilling and peaceful existence through honest introspection and ongoing self-care."

Courage in Love's Simplicity

"Courage in love is not about grand gestures but in the simple act of being fully present."

Dissolve the Fog

"Clarity in communication dissolves the fog of assumptions, allowing genuine connection and deeper bonds to flourish."

Divine Creation

"A mother's love is the creation of the Divine, a living testament to compassion and kindness, bringing peace to the world."

Divine Illumination

"Your glory illuminates the heavens, each star and planet bowing in reverence to your divine grace."

Echoes of Cherished Love Quote

"Her concern for my happiness echoes through the night, a gentle reminder that I am cherished beyond measure, regardless of circumstance."

Embrace Each Thread

"In the tapestry of human connection, each thread represents a unique perspective. To truly understand the beauty of the whole, we must honour and embrace each thread."

Embrace the Present

"The present moment is the only place where life truly unfolds; embrace it, and love will find its way."

Embracing Imperfection

"Love is not just a feeling; it is a courageous choice to see the beauty in imperfection and embrace the vulnerability of our hearts."

Empowerment through Acceptance

"To love oneself means accepting every aspect of yourself, both light and shadow. True self-acceptance turns self-doubt into empowerment."

Endless River

"A mother's love is a river of compassion, flowing endlessly through life's trials, nurturing and sustaining those she cherishes."

Experience the Fullness

"In the quiet of the present, we find the profound; to be present is to experience the fullness of love and life."

Firm amidst Storms Quote

"Through the storms of life, her love stands firm, a beacon of constancy amidst the chaos, guiding me with its pure and sublime essence."

Fractured Yet Whole

"A cracked vase doesn't lose its purpose; it becomes a testament to the hands that hold it together."

Gateway to Profound Love

"Accepting yourself is not about perfection; it's about embracing your imperfections with compassion. This acceptance is the gateway to a more profound and lasting self-love."

Gift of Presence

"Presence is the gift we give ourselves and others; it's where genuine connection and true appreciation reside."

Heavenly Affection

"I have not seen the Divine, but in my mother's affection and her gentle feet, I have found heaven on earth."

Home in Unconditional Love

"In the arms of unconditional love, we find a home where our flaws are not just accepted, but cherished—a place where we are loved, not despite who we are, but because of it."

Illuminate the Beauty of Now

"To love deeply is to be fully present; when we let go of yesterday's shadows and tomorrow's fears, we illuminate the beauty of now."

Infinite Possibilities

"The magic of life is found in the here and now; we can unleash the infinite possibilities of joy and love by living fully in the present."The Quiet of Compassion: "Even in the ruins of a shattered bond, love can find its way—not to rekindle, but to heal."

Key to Fulfilment

"When we fully accept who we are, we allow ourselves to grow and prosper. Acceptance of oneself is the key to living a life of genuine love and fulfilment."

Love Beyond Conditions

"True love does not cling, demand, or possess—it flows like a river, nourishing everything in its path, yet never asking the land to hold it captive."

Love Beyond Logic

"When you are in love, logic becomes a distant whisper, and words stumble in the presence of emotions too profound for language to hold."

Love as a Transformative Force

"Love is not just a feeling but a transformative force that heals wounds, bridges divides, and illuminates the darkest corners of our souls."

Mindfulness Amidst Chaos

"Amidst the chaos of the world, mindfulness becomes our anchor, grounding us in the present moment where we discover the profound beauty and serenity of simply being."

Nourishing Bloom

"In the garden of self-love, self-acceptance is the soil that nourishes the bloom. Without it, our potential remains unfulfilled, and our heart remains guarded."

Nurturing Love

"Love, like a garden, requires daily attention. It flourishes with open communication, shared experiences, and unwavering support, blooming more beautifully as it's nurtured over time."

Nurturing Unwavering Support Quote

"Her love sees beyond my faults, nurturing my spirit with pride and guidance, a testament to the depth of her unwavering support."

On Self-Compassion

"To love oneself is the beginning of a lifelong romance. Embrace your imperfections, for they are the unique brushstrokes on the canvas of your soul, painting a masterpiece of resilience and grace."

On Unconditional Love and Acceptance

"Unconditional love is the bridge between our hearts and the world's suffering, a light that dispels the shadows of judgment and fear. It is in loving without limits that we find the truest essence of our humanity."

On the Beauty of Compassion

"Compassion is the heartbeat of humanity, a gentle pulse that reminds us of our interconnectedness. In every act of kindness, we breathe life into the world, creating ripples of hope that touch souls far and wide."

On the Gift of Presence

"In the quiet moments of presence, we find the essence of connection. Just being with another, without demands or expectations, allows love to bloom in the sacred space between hearts."

On the Impact of Empathy

"Empathy is the silent thread that weaves our souls together, a gentle reminder that beneath our differences lies a shared humanity. In understanding another's pain, we find the strength to heal our own."

On the Transformative Power of Love

"Love is the alchemy that transforms our lives, turning ordinary moments into extraordinary memories. It is a force that defies logic, a magic that can heal the deepest wounds and bring light to the darkest corners of our hearts."

Open Doors

"To assume is to build walls between hearts; to communicate is to open doors to understanding."

Purpose of Conversation

"Remember that the purpose of any conversation is to understand rather than to be correct. True connection arises when we acknowledge and validate the various experiences that define each individual's reality."

Quiet Strength Quote

"In her quiet strength, she shields me from her own pain, selflessly bearing burdens so that my path remains clear and unburdened."

Radiant Sanctuary

"The light of my mother's love outshines the brightest star, her presence a sanctuary where I find solace and strength."

Resilience in Reflection

"In the reflection of my past, I see the shadows of pain and regret; but in the mirror of today, I see the resilience and wisdom that have shaped who I am."

Resilience in Silence

"Silence is not surrender; it's a quiet rebellion, a choice to rise above the noise. In its stillness, the heart learns to endure, to heal, and to thrive."

Revitalising Relationships

"Just as sunlight revives a garden, quality time revitalises a relationship. Love strengthens and grows during these moments of mutual joy and connection."

Sacred Gift

"In every sacrifice she makes, my mother weaves a tapestry of love, her selflessness a sacred gift that shapes my existence."

Seeds of Renewal

"Healing begins when we stop watering the roots of regret and start planting seeds of understanding."

Strength in Diversity

"The strength of a relationship lies not in the sameness of perspectives but in the respect and appreciation of each other's unique views."

Strength in Shadows

"True strength is not found in loud victories but in the quiet resolve to rise each day, even when the world feels like an unbearable weight."

Strength in Silence

"True strength isn't in the loudness of a fight but in the quiet grace of enduring what the heart should not have to."

Strength of the Unseen Bond

"The strongest ties aren't woven by blood but by the trust we place in one another when everything else seems to crumble."

Symphony of Beauty and Benevolence

"Celestial melodies and floral aromas blend into a symphony of your boundless beauty and benevolence."

The Chains of Fear in Love

"When fear holds us back from love, we chain our hearts to loneliness."

The Choice to Anchor

"In every storm, there are two choices—to drift with the current or to anchor yourself to what matters most. The anchor is heavier, but it's the only way to survive."

The Echo of Endurance

"Silence is not the absence of a voice but the presence of a storm. In its quiet fury, it shapes the strongest souls, carving resilience from despair."

The Echo of Love

"Love is not measured by how much we receive, but by how deeply we give. The echo of true love is not in words spoken, but in hearts touched."

The Echo of Purpose

"Purpose is not a destination; it's the quiet echo of your soul finding harmony with the world. It isn't something you chase—it's something you uncover in the work, the struggle, and the moments you almost give up."

The Essence of Unconditional Love

"Unconditional love is the light that remains when all else fades, a quiet force that embraces without judgment and heals without asking for anything in return."

The Fleeting Nature of Love

"Time may be abundant, but love is fleeting; cherish the moments before they become memories."

The Fragility of Trust

"Trust is not broken in one blow but chipped away by whispers of doubt and unspoken truths."

The Journey of Self-Love

"In the quiet embrace of solitude, I discovered that self-love is not a destination but a journey—a gentle unfolding of the heart, where I learn to be my sanctuary and the source of my light."

The Language of the Soul

"Love renders words powerless and reason irrelevant, as the soul speaks a language only the heart can translate."

The Light of Unconditional Love

"Unconditional love is the light that dissolves the shadows of fear and judgment, illuminating the path to deeper connections and boundless compassion. It is in the embrace of this love that we discover the true essence of our humanity."

The Love That Waits

"A mother's love never leaves—it lingers in the air we breathe, in the lessons we carry, and in the silence where we finally understand."

The Mirror of Insecurities

"Jealousy doesn't see the truth; it only sees a warped reflection of its own fears."

The Mirror of Pain

"Sometimes, the faces of those we love become mirrors, reflecting the wounds we refused to see in ourselves."

The Price of Delayed Love

"Love delayed is love denied—give fully today, for tomorrow is never promised."

The Priceless Gift of Presence

"Presence is the greatest gift we can give to those we love; time is precious, but love is priceless."

The Quiet Revolution of Self-Love

"Self-love is the quiet revolution within, where we tenderly reclaim our worth and write a narrative of compassion and resilience, transforming every wound into a testament of our strength."

The Quiet Whisper of Self-Love

"True self-love is the quiet acceptance of both your flaws and your successes. It's the whisper that says, 'You are enough,' and the unwavering certainty that your value is innate and infinite."

The Rhythms of Love

"In love's embrace, sanity becomes a shadow, for the heart beats to rhythms the mind can never fully understand."

The Sanctuary of Self-Love

"In the sanctuary of self-love, we find the strength to embrace our imperfections and celebrate our uniqueness, creating a life woven with the threads of authenticity and grace."

The Sorrow of Unloved Moments

"The greatest sorrow is not losing someone we love, but realising we never fully loved them when we had the chance."

The Storm Within

"Jealousy is a quiet storm; it doesn't announce itself with thunder but grows in whispers, until its winds tear through everything you thought was safe."

The Unseen Road Ahead

"Growth is not the absence of fear, but the willingness to walk forward despite it. The road may be unfamiliar, but every step reveals a piece of who you are meant to become."

The Warrior Within

"My life's journey is etched with scars, each a reminder of the battles I've faced, yet in the mirror, I find the warrior who has conquered them all."

The Weight of Belief

"Sometimes, belief from another is the bridge you need to find faith in yourself. It's in their unwavering trust that you begin to see your potential."

The Weight of Insecurity

"Jealousy is a mirror that reflects only what we fear to lose, not what we truly hold."

The Weight of Love

"Love isn't a fragile thread but a chain forged in fire—unbreakable yet heavy. It demands strength to carry, but in its weight lies the power to hold everything together."

The Weight of Redemption

"The heaviest chains are the ones we forge in our hearts, and breaking them takes more courage than facing the world's fiercest storms."

The Weight of Responsibility

"There comes a moment when silence becomes heavier than truth, and speaking it feels like standing against a storm—but some storms are worth facing for the sake of what's right."

The Weight of Silence

"Sometimes, the heaviest burden isn't the truth we know, but the fear of what it will break when we speak it."

The Weight of Unspoken Words

"Regret is the weight of unspoken words and untouched hearts; love while you still have the chance."

Triumph Over Heartache

"The path behind me is littered with heartache and mistakes, yet when I face myself, I see the triumph of enduring and the quiet pride of having grown stronger."

True Success Lies in Love

"Success without love is an empty victory; true wealth is found in the hearts we touch."

Unconditional Cocoon

"In my mother's embrace, I feel the touch of the divine, her warmth and care enveloping me in a cocoon of unconditional love."

Universe in a Keepsake

"The keepsake you gave me holds a universe of shared moments, connecting us across the vast distances of life."

Unspoken Love, the Deepest Regret

"The deepest regret comes not from what we did, but from the love we left unspoken."

Whisper on the Wind

"Your presence, like a whisper on the wind, carries the weight of unspoken love and cherished memories."

"Forgiveness in the Light"

"To forgive another is an act of grace; to forgive oneself is a battle against shadows only the brave dare to fight."

Serenity and Balance

Cultivating Inner Peace

"Balance is not about holding everything together—it's about knowing what to hold and what to release. In letting go of control, we make room for grace."

- *Shree Shambav*

A Breath of Peace

"Each breath taken in silence is a step toward peace, a moment of pure, unfiltered being."

A Fresh Canvas at Dawn

"In the canvas of each dawn lies a fresh palette, painted only by the courage to begin again."

A Journey Back Home

"The journey into silence is the journey home—to the essence of who we are beneath all that we do."

A Journey to Wholeness

"To seek silence is to seek communion with the self, a path that leads to wholeness and healing."

A Pilgrimage Within

"The journey to self-discovery is not a search outside ourselves but a pilgrimage within."

Beyond the World's Noise

"Each moment of silence is a gentle reminder that we are not defined by the world's noise."

Breathing Space for the Spirit

"Silence is the space where our spirit breathes, expanding in peace, insight, and freedom."

Bridges of Compassion

"When pride builds walls, love builds bridges, and through those bridges, even broken hearts can find their way home."

Catalyst for Personal Growth

"Silence is not merely an absence of sound; it is a powerful catalyst for self-liberation, providing the stillness needed to dismantle mental clutter and societal pressures, revealing a pathway to personal growth and a more fulfilling existence."

Clearing the Path to Clarity

"The path to clarity is not in accumulating knowledge but in shedding the illusions that cloud our vision."

Connection as the True Measure

"The real measure of success is not in how high you climb, but in how deeply you connect—with yourself, with others, and with the present moment."

Courage in the Unknown

"In the stillness of your heart, you'll find the courage to embrace life's uncertainties with grace, for it is within the unknown that the seeds of transformation are sown."

Discovering Inner Wholeness

"In the vast expanse of quiet, we come to realise that we are already whole."

Echoes of True Desire

"In embracing silence, we hear the echoes of our own desires, unfiltered by the world's expectations."

Embracing Duality with Grace

"Strength is not the absence of weakness, but the courage to rise and embrace both with grace."

Fertile Ground for Self-Discovery

"Silence can be daunting, a mirror reflecting our deepest fears and insecurities. Yet, when we dare to embrace it, we discover that within this void lies a fertile ground for self-discovery—a powerful invitation to connect with our true selves and find strength in stillness."

Forged in the Fires of Challenge

"Embrace each challenge as a chapter in the story of becoming, for it is only through fire that steel is forged."

Freedom Beyond Illusion

"True freedom is not in escaping the world but in realising that nothing in the world can bind you."

Healing Through Release

"Healing begins when we let go of the stories that no longer serve us, allowing space for new light to enter."

Illuminated Within

"Like the stars that shine only in the dark, our inner light reveals itself in the quiet."

Keys to Liberation in Silence

"In the embrace of silence, we find the keys to our own liberation, allowing us to step away from the cacophony of expectations and discover the whispers of our authentic selves—a sanctuary where true desires and values can flourish."

Kindness

A Quiet Force: "Kindness is the quiet force that transforms the world, one small act at a time. It ripples through hearts, lighting the way for others to find compassion within themselves, creating a tapestry of love that binds us all together."

Lessons in Stillness

"Life whispers lessons in each moment of stillness; the louder we live, the softer they sound."

Life's Sacred Rhythm

"In silence, we learn to witness life unfolding, not as spectators but as part of its sacred rhythm."

Listening to the Soul's Whispers

"Growth begins when we stop seeking validation from others and start listening to the whispers of our soul."

Love in Presence, Not Words

"Love is not a grand gesture; it is the quiet, consistent presence that nurtures souls and transforms hearts without a single word."

Reconnecting with Life's Beat

"In silence, we reconnect with the rhythm of life, hearing its gentle beat within our hearts."

Reflections of a Still Mind

"The calmest waters reflect the clearest skies—so too does a still mind reflect the depths of the soul."

Resilience Through Crisis

"During times of crisis, silence is a strong ally, offering us the stillness we need to ponder and recalibrate. By accepting this silence, we grow resilience and emotional equilibrium, transforming upheaval into an opportunity for profound introspection and regeneration."

Resilience Through Loss

"True strength is not in the battles we win, but in the quiet resilience we cultivate through our losses."

Resilience Through the Cracks

"The beauty of resilience is in the cracks—through them, we find our way to the light."

Roots of Resilience

"Resilience is not just weathering the storm but growing roots deep enough to bloom within it."

Sanctuary of the Soul

"When we embrace silence, we open the door to a sanctuary within, untouched by the chaos of the world."

Self-Acceptance Over Applause

"A heart that knows itself need not seek validation in the echo of others' applause."

Shaped by the Storms

"We grow not by avoiding the storms, but by learning to stand tall amidst them, knowing that every gust of wind shapes us into who we are meant to become."

Simplicity's Secret

"Silence reveals the beauty of simplicity, a reminder that the truest answers lie in the quietest places."

Strength in Silence

"In the quiet resilience of a battered soul lies a strength louder than the roars of anger or the cries of despair."

Strength in Surrender

"Sometimes the greatest strength lies in our willingness to surrender to what we cannot control."

The Courage to Be Quiet

"In a world that demands noise, finding silence is an act of courage and a return to oneself."

The Courageous Journey Inward

"Confronting the discomfort of silence is not an act of avoidance, but a courageous journey inward. By reframing our relationship with silence, we unlock its potential as a profound teacher, guiding us to introspection, growth, and a deeper harmony with the world around us."

The Creative Stillness

"The stillness within you is not empty; it is the wellspring of creation, echoing with the heartbeat of existence."

The Dance of Life

"Life is not about chasing what you desire, but about flowing with the rhythm of existence, surrendering to its mysteries without resistance."

The Depth in Every Quiet Moment

"Beneath the surface of every quiet moment lies a world of depth, waiting to be discovered."

The Divine Within

"The divine does not dwell in distant heavens, but in the silent chambers of your heart, waiting for you to notice."

The Echoes of Stillness

"In the stillness of silence, we find echoes of truths too profound for words."

The Flame of the Infinite

"The soul is not a fragment but a flame of the infinite; its light dances in the cosmos, yet it resides quietly within."

The Form of Solace

"If solace had a form, it would take shape in your embrace—a sanctuary where chaos unravels and the weary soul finds its quiet home."

The Fullness of Silence

"In a world of noise, silence is not emptiness; it is the fullness of presence."

The Fullness of True Silence

"True silence is not an emptiness but a fullness—a presence that calls us back to ourselves."

The Garden of Inner Clarity

"Silence is the garden where clarity blooms, where seeds of insight are planted and nourished."

The Gift of Simplicity

"The beauty of silence lies in its simplicity—it holds nothing yet offers everything."

The Greatest Conquest

"You may conquer lands, wealth, and men, but the fiercest battle is within. Master yourself, and the world will bow without force."

The Heart of Truth

"Truth is not a concept to be learned, but a realisation that comes when we silence the noise of the world and listen to the wisdom within."

The Heart's Canvas

"Silence is the canvas upon which the heart paints its deepest truths, unbound by words."

The Heart's Quiet Voice

"Listen to the spaces between thoughts, for there the heart speaks its clearest truths."

The Hidden Answers of Stillness

"In the stillness of silence, we find answers to questions we didn't know we were asking."

The Journey Home

"We wander far in search of treasures, only to realise that what we long for was never beyond us, but within."

The Journey Inward

"In the stillness of your heart lies a profound truth: that the journey inward is far more rewarding than the path that leads outward."

The Language Beyond Words

"In silence, we discover the language of the heart, a language beyond words and thoughts."

The Language of Silence

"In the quiet of our souls, we find truths that no words can carry, and in those truths, we find ourselves."

The Measure of Power

"True power is not in the wealth we hoard, nor in the fear we inspire, but in the lives we uplift when we have nothing to gain."

The Measure of Riches

"A man's wealth is not measured by what he hoards, but by what he gives away without hesitation."

The Paradox of Giving

"A hand that gives is never empty, for generosity is the only treasure that multiplies when shared."

The Patient Companion

"Silence is the companion that patiently awaits our presence, inviting us to listen deeply and live fully."

The Peace of Being

"When we rest in silence, we discover the profound peace of simply being."

The Peace of Letting Go

"To surrender is not to lose, but to gain. When we release what weighs us down, we make room for the peace that is our birthright."

The Power of the Right Questions

"True wisdom begins not when we have all the answers, but when we are brave enough to ask the right questions."

The Quiet Path to Wisdom

"The quieter we become, the more we hear—the whispers of the universe, the wisdom of the soul."

The Quiet Song of Peace

"Success is not in the things we acquire, but in the peace we cultivate within, where all external noise fades and the quiet voice of our heart becomes the loudest song."

The Renewal Within the Pause

"Every pause holds a chance for renewal, an invitation to come back to ourselves before moving forward."

The Return to Light

"To align consciousness with wholeness is to let the scattered fragments of the self return to the light of their origin. In that union, we rediscover our essence, where every wound becomes wisdom and every shadow dissolves into peace."

The Richness of Simplicity

"In the quiet moments of simplicity, we find the richness of life. It is in the unadorned, everyday things that the soul recognises its deepest joy—where peace thrives and beauty whispers softly, urging us to slow down and embrace the present."

The River of Peace

"While happiness flickers like fire, peace flows like a river. The wise do not chase sparks; they learn to swim."

The Road Back to Oneself

"Some journeys take us across lands and seas, but the greatest journey is the one that leads us back to who we were meant to be."

The Sacred Rhythm

"Every heartbeat is an echo of the universal rhythm; to live mindfully is to hear its sacred song."

The Silence of the Soul

"In the silence between thoughts, in the spaces between breaths, we find our truest selves—where time ceases to exist, and the soul whispers its deepest truths."

The Silent Infinite

"Emptiness is not the absence of being but the presence of infinite potential. It is the quiet canvas where the universe paints its masterpiece."

The Silent Revolution of Inner Transformation

"By choosing silence, we begin a journey of inner transformation—a 'silent revolution' that gently reshapes our lives. In the stillness, we regain clarity, peace, and a deeper connection to ourselves, allowing us to live life to its fullest, most balanced form."

The Silent Teacher

"Wisdom does not always come from the mouths of kings and scholars—sometimes, it whispers through the innocent laughter of a child."

The Soul's Quiet Dialogue

"The language of the soul is spoken in silence, where the heart's desires are laid bare and understood."

The Source of Love

"Love is not a commodity to be obtained, but the very essence that flows through us when we let go of all expectations and attachments."

The Stillness Within

"When consciousness rests in its natural state of wholeness, the turbulence of life fades. In that stillness, healing emerges—not as an effort, but as the gentle unfolding of what was always complete."

The Strength of Silence

"In moments of silence, we find the strength to step back, to observe without judgment, and to let go."

The Symphony of Being

"Aligning consciousness with wholeness is like tuning a forgotten melody within. In the harmony of mind, body, and spirit, the soul's symphony plays the music of healing."

The Teacher Called Pain

"Suffering is not life's punishment, but its whisper. Those who listen find wisdom; those who resist remain lost."

The Unseen Force of Silence

"Silence is the unseen force that can reshape our existence. As we weave it into our daily routines, we uncover its profound ability to nurture growth, deepen connections, and awaken a sense of fulfilment that only stillness can offer."

The Unspoken Language of Strength

"When words fall short, silence speaks—a language of the heart that fills us with a quiet, unwavering strength."

The Vessel of Truth

"In emptiness lies the essence of truth, for only when the vessel is unfilled can it receive the boundless streams of love, peace, and wisdom."

The Voice of Solace

"If solace had a voice, it would echo your name—steady, gentle, and endlessly soothing, a reminder that peace is not a place but a presence."

The Weight of Resilience

"Strength isn't measured by what you endure; it's revealed in how you rebuild after being broken."

The Whisper of the Soul

"Essence is emptiness—a sacred stillness where the soul listens to the echoes of the divine. In surrendering to it, we become whole."

The Wisdom of Letting Go

"Letting go is not weakness; it is the wisdom to understand what truly belongs."

The Wisdom of Quiet Presence

"Silence is not the absence of sound, but the presence of wisdom waiting to be heard."

The Wisdom of Silence

"Silence is not an absence, but a presence. It is in the quiet that the heart hears the whispers of the divine, guiding us back to ourselves."

Treasure in the Small Pleasures

"The beauty of simplicity lies not in the absence of complexity, but in the clarity it brings. When we pause to savour life's small pleasures, we uncover treasures hidden in plain sight, reminding us that true happiness is found in what is simple and pure."

True Peace Within

"True peace is found not in the absence of challenges, but in the presence of a still mind."

Unmasking the Self

"Silence is the sanctuary where we meet ourselves, raw and unguarded, beyond the masks we wear."

Unravelling the World's Noise

"In the embrace of silence, we unravel the noise of the world and connect to the voice of our own truth."

Unwavering in the Winds

"A person rooted in their values stands unwavering, even as the winds of life blow strong."

Wisdom Beyond Boundaries

"True wisdom is not the accumulation of knowledge but the dissolution of the boundaries between self and the eternal."

Shades of Existence

Light of life

"Do not fear your shadow—it is proof that the light exists behind you. Every sorrow you carry is a contour of the life you've dared to live."

- *Shree Shambav*

A Fleeting Gift

"Death teaches us that every moment is a fleeting gift, reminding us to live with purpose, to love with abandon, and to embrace change with the grace of knowing it is all part of the grand tapestry of existence."

A New Beginning Beyond the Physical

"Death is not the final chapter but the turning of a page—an invitation for the soul to journey beyond the confines of the physical."

A Spiral Path to Truth

"The spiritual journey is a spiral, not a straight line, drawing us ever deeper into the heart of truth, where each return to the same question reveals a deeper understanding of who we are."

A Threshold of Awakening

"Death is not an end but a threshold—a passage where the soul is gently guided toward its next stage of awakening, embraced by light, love, and a timeless wisdom."

Architects of Destiny

"In the realm of possibilities, faith and persistent contemplation are the architects of destiny. Hold your desires in your heart with unwavering belief, and you will become what you envision."

Attuning to Higher Frequencies

"When we attune our consciousness to higher frequencies, we connect with the greater cosmic flow, harmonising ourselves with the universe and accelerating our spiritual evolution."

Awakening Vitality Within

"To heal is not to fix what is broken but to awaken the infinite flow of vitality and harmony within."

Awakening as a Gentle Unfolding

"Awakening is not a final arrival, but a continual process of shedding illusions, each step a gentle unfolding into the truth of our eternal nature."

Awakening to True Life

"To die before death is to surrender to fear and stagnation. True life begins when we cast off the shackles of self-doubt and live with purpose, embracing each moment as if it were our first breath."

Beyond the Physical Realm

"Life beyond the physical realm is not a distant place, but a state of being—where the soul sheds the limitations of the body and expands into the boundless truths of existence."

Beyond the Tangible Evidence

"Evidence is not just found in the tangible—it is in the quiet moments when the soul recognises a truth beyond words, an experience that transcends the limits of the physical world."

Consciousness

The Fabric of Reality: "Consciousness is not a passive observer of reality, but the very fabric through which the universe is woven, shaping our experiences, perceptions, and the reality we live within."

Cosmic Reflections

"In the quiet embrace of the stars, we find the echoes of our deepest desires and fears. The cosmos is not a distant realm but a mirror reflecting the labyrinth of our souls."

Death

The Wise Teacher: "Death is not a foe to fear, but a wise teacher who guides us to understand the impermanence of life, the preciousness of each moment, and the eternal truths that lie beyond the physical realm."

Death as a Door to Infinite Horizons

"Death is not the end of the soul but the opening of a door to infinite horizons where consciousness continues to evolve."

Destiny Through Focus

"The power to shape your destiny lies in the persistent focus of your thoughts and the steadfastness of your faith. Envision your desires with clarity and conviction, and watch as the universe aligns to make them real."

Embracing the Mystery

"To understand death is to glimpse the infinite; it is in surrendering to the mystery that we begin to truly understand life."

Exploring the Unknown

"In the pursuit of understanding the afterlife, science does not seek to dismiss the unknown but to explore it—offering a bridge between the tangible world and the mysteries that transcend it."

Faith as Sculptor

"The power of belief transforms dreams into reality and shadows into light. Man is sculpted by his faith, and as he believes, his world takes shape and meaning."

Finding Guidance in the Stillness of the Mind

"In the stillness of the mind, consciousness finds its voice. It is in this space that true guidance, peace, and self-realisation emerge."

Guiding Stars

"Your love and precious memories are now our guiding stars, lighting the way through the deep void your absence has left in our souls."

Harvesting Destiny

"The seeds of our destiny are sown in the fertile soil of the present, nurtured by the choices we make and the love we cultivate. What we harvest is not a mere reflection of fate, but a testament to our enduring spirit."

Honouring the Courage of Transformation

"To embrace transformation is to honour the courage it takes to shed the old and step boldly into the infinite potential of the self."

Igniting the Flame Within

"Inspiration ignites the spark within, a gentle reminder of the greatness we often forget resides in us. Motivation fans that flame, urging us to rise above doubts, embrace our purpose, and walk boldly toward the life we were meant to create."

Illuminating the Path

"Perform your duties with sincerity and passion, for it is in action that we truly live. Inaction leads to stagnation, but purposeful deeds illuminate our path and define our legacy."

Intuition

The Sacred Bridge to Truth: "Intuition is the sacred bridge between the seen and unseen, guiding us toward the truth that logic alone cannot unveil."

Karma and Evolution

"Karma is not merely the sum of our actions, but the ripple of intention, guiding the soul's evolution through lifetimes—each choice an opportunity to align more deeply with our true nature."

Keeper of Mysteries

"Time is a silent keeper of mysteries, folding the past into shadows and the future into veils, urging us to seek meaning in the fleeting present."

Listening to Time's Whispers

"In the endless flow of time, mysteries hide like whispers in the wind, revealing their truths only to those who listen with patience and an open heart."

Living Without Regret

"Don't let the weight of regret, unfulfilled dreams, or untapped potential bury you while you still breathe. Live fully, love deeply, and chase your passions with fierce determination—don't die a little each day waiting for the end."

Love Beyond Time and Space

"Communication with the departed is not bound by time or space; it is a silent exchange of love, a reminder that those we've lost are never truly gone, but merely waiting in another form."

Moments of Timeless Unity

"Moments of timeless unity reveal the sacred tapestry of existence, reminding us that beyond the noise of life lies a boundless reservoir of peace, wisdom, and connection."

Purpose Born from Inner Truth

"Purpose is not found in the outer world but created within—when our actions align with the timeless truth of who we are."

Purpose in Every Thread

"In the grand tapestry of life, every thread holds purpose and meaning. There is nothing lost or wasted, for even our smallest moments weave together to create the beautiful story of our existence."

Purposeful Living

"Fulfil your responsibilities with unwavering dedication, for it is through action that we find purpose and meaning. In the stillness of inaction, dreams fade, but through our efforts, they come alive."

Reality as a Reflection of Consciousness

"Reality is not an external truth waiting to be uncovered, but a reflection of our consciousness, where the seen reveals the unseen and the tangible dissolves into the mystical."

Reflection of Life

"Philosophy teaches us that death is not an enemy to be conquered but a mystery to be understood—a mirror reflecting the meaning we give to life."

Reflections of Eternal Truths

"The universe whispers its secrets through the act of creation, revealing that every form is a reflection of eternal truths. What we bring into existence is merely the tangible expression of the profound realities already present within."

Reincarnation

A Silent Thread: "Reincarnation is not merely a concept but a silent thread woven through the tapestry of existence, where the soul reawakens, carrying the lessons of its past and the potential of its future in every new life."

Rhythm of Action

"In the dance of life, action is the rhythm that keeps us moving forward. Embrace your duties with a full heart, for through purposeful action, we weave the fabric of our destiny."

Sacred Pages of Existence

"Each moment is a sacred page in the book of our existence, written by the hands of the universe. Embrace the wisdom of the past, for it is the ink that guides the pen of your future."

Science and Spirituality United

"Science seeks to understand the mechanics of existence, while spirituality reveals its deeper meaning; together, they offer a holistic view of life's mysteries, where the seen and unseen are two sides of the same truth."

Shaping Reality with Thought

"The boundaries of reality are not fixed—they are the malleable creation of our consciousness, where every thought and intention sends ripples into the fabric of existence, sculpting the world we encounter."

Stairway of Tears

"If tears could build a stairway and memories pave a path, we would journey to where you are, bridging the divide to find solace with our lost angel."

Stardust in Motion

"As the celestial dance unfolds above, so too dances our lives beneath. We are but stardust in motion, crafting our constellations amidst the vast, ever-changing sky of existence."

Stepping Into the Infinite

"In the moments after death, the soul steps into a realm where time dissolves, and the essence of who we are is revealed, unburdened by the constraints of the body."

The Architect of Destiny

"A man's belief shapes his destiny, carving his path with the chisel of conviction. As he believes, so he becomes, for faith is the architect of the soul's journey."

The Bridge to Oneness

"In the oneness of all life, we discover that love is the bridge, and unity is the destination."

The Crossroads of the Soul

"In the interlife, the soul stands at the crossroads of its past and future, choosing not only the lessons it will carry forward but also the path of growth it will follow toward enlightenment."

The Cycle of Transformation

"In nature's embrace, death is but a transformation—a fallen leaf becomes the soil, a reminder that endings nourish new beginnings."

The Dance Between Perception and Existence

"When we see through the lens of consciousness, reality becomes a malleable dance between perception and existence, a realm where the boundaries of the material world fade into the infinite."

The Echoes of Reincarnation

"The evidence of reincarnation is not always found in facts, but in the echoes of memories that stir deep within us—whispers of lives we've lived and the souls we've known, beyond the veils of time."

The End of Suffering

"Suffering arises when we cling to what is fleeting. When we learn to release our attachments, we transcend pain and step into the freedom of the present moment."

The Essence of Consciousness

"To understand consciousness is to touch the very essence of existence; it is the bridge between the known and the mysterious, the observer and the observed."

The Essence of True Connection

"The actual essence of connection is not the number of interactions, but the quality of the links we cultivate. Our lives grow, like a garden, when we develop meaningful interactions, sowing seeds of trust and nurturing them with empathy and care."

The Eternal Dance

"Death is not the opposite of life but the rhythm between endings and beginnings—an eternal dance where consciousness transcends the boundaries of form."

The Eternal Rhythm

"After death, the soul returns to the eternal rhythm of nature, like a river merging back into the ocean, endless yet ever-present."

The Great Equalizer

"Death is the great equaliser, not because it takes all things away, but because it reveals what truly matters—the spirit's eternal dance with the mysteries of existence."

The Heartbeat of Life

"Passion is the heartbeat of a life well-lived; it's the echo of your soul's deepest desires, guiding you through the mundane and into the realm of extraordinary fulfilment."

The Heart's Unseen Truths

"The deepest experiences are not those we can measure with science, but those we feel in the heart—where the unseen world speaks to us, whispering of truths too vast for the mind to grasp."

The Illusion of Clocks

"The clock ticks not for time itself, but for the illusion we've built to tame eternity within the boundaries of our understanding."

The Infinite Awakening

"The journey of the soul is not toward a final resting place, but toward the awakening of the infinite potential within, where liberation from the cycle of rebirth reveals the eternal truth of our existence."

The Infinite Passage

"To the body, death is an ending; to the soul, it is but a moment of passage, like stepping through a doorway into a broader, infinite existence."

The Intersection of Science and Spirit

"When science and spirituality converge, they reveal that the laws of the universe are not only governed by physics but also by consciousness, reminding us that the cosmos is as much a spiritual experience as it is a scientific one."

The Journey Inward

"The greatest journey is not outward, but inward. It is through self-inquiry that we discover the vastness of our own being, a journey that leads to eternal peace."

The Journey of Conscious Evolution

"Conscious evolution is the soul's journey toward greater awareness, where every thought, every deed, shapes not just our future, but the very essence of who we are becoming."

The Joy of Being

"True joy does not come from what we acquire or achieve, but from the simple act of being—being present, being aware, and being alive."

The Legacy of Love

"In facing death, we come to understand that what we leave behind is not material wealth, but the love we've shared, the wisdom we've imparted, and the marks we've made on the souls of those we've touched."

The Liberation of Emptiness

"Emptiness is not a void to be feared, but a space to be embraced. It is within this vast silence that we are liberated from the illusions of the world."

The Loudest Truths

"In the silence of death, we find the loudest truths—truths about love, loss, and the boundless journey of the soul that transcends time and space."

The Mind as a Servant to Consciousness

"The mind is not the master, but a servant to consciousness. True spiritual growth begins when we quiet the mind and allow the wisdom of the soul to guide us."

The Mirage of Time

"Time is a mirage, a construct of the mind, blurring the infinite now into past and future, yet reality dwells only in the stillness of the present."

The Mirror of the Mind

"The mind reflects the world, but the soul reflects the truth. Clean the mirror of your thoughts, and you will see the divine radiance within."

The Oneness of All

"All that exists is woven from the same thread of consciousness. In understanding the unity of all things, we recognise that to harm another is to harm ourselves."

The Path of Awakening

"The soul's journey is not a path of distance but of awakening—a return to the divine, guided by the wisdom of countless lifetimes and the teachings of the spirit."

The Present as Truth

"Time is an illusion we chase, measuring the immeasurable, while the present moment remains the only truth we ever truly possess."

The Reunion with the Eternal

"Mystical encounters at the time of death remind us that the end is not a solitary journey but a reunion with the eternal, where the soul is met by the light of love and divine presence."

The Sacred Interlife

"The interlife is not a pause, but a sacred space of reflection and choice, where the soul reviews its past and consciously shapes its next journey, guided by the wisdom it has gained."

The Sacred Odyssey

"Across every tradition, the soul's journey is a sacred odyssey—each life a step, each death a pause, and each rebirth a chance to move closer to the truth of who we are."

The Silent Whisper of Love

"In the stillness of the soul, the departed speak not through words, but through signs, dreams, and subtle whispers, teaching us that the bond of love transcends the boundaries of life and death."

The Soul's Ultimate Destination

"The soul's ultimate destination is not a place, but a state of being—where the boundaries between self and the divine dissolve, and all that remains is the pure essence of love and unity."

The Tapestry of Destiny

"Life's journey is a tapestry woven from the threads of fate and free will. We may not control the patterns of our destiny, but we hold the loom that shapes our response to its intricate design."

The Tapestry of Life and Death

"Every culture weaves its tapestry of death, threading rituals, beliefs, and symbols to make sense of the unknown, reminding us that death is as much about the living as it is about the departed."

The Threshold

"What we call death is merely a threshold; for some, it is an end, and for others, the dawn of a vast and boundless beginning."

The Tragedy of a Half-Lived Life

"Death is unavoidable, but a life half-lived is a tragedy. Refuse to die in spirit before your body; instead, embrace growth, challenge, and change until your last breath."

The Transformative Energy of Consciousness

"Consciousness is the energy that flows through us, shaping the vibrations we send into the world. Aligning our energy with love, compassion, and wisdom transforms both our inner and outer realities."

The True Reality

"The physical world is but a shadow of the true reality; beyond it lies a vast, infinite realm where consciousness transcends time and space, and the soul finds its eternal home."

The Truth of Nature

"In death, nature whispers the ultimate truth: nothing truly vanishes; everything evolves, returning to the infinite cycle of creation and renewal."

The Ultimate Frontier

"The afterlife, though elusive to the senses, may be the ultimate frontier for science—where the laws of physics meet the realm of consciousness, challenging us to expand our understanding of existence beyond the body."

The Veil Between Worlds

"In the final moments of life, the veil between worlds thins, and deathbed visions become a doorway—offering glimpses of those we have loved and those who guide us to the next realm."

The Whisper of Truth

"In the quiet chambers of the heart, where the world cannot intrude, lies a truth so profound it defies words—a whisper of the infinite, calling us to remember who we are."

The Wisdom of Intuitive Whispers

"The whispers of intuition carry the wisdom of the infinite, inviting us to trust the path only the soul can see."

Transcending Self to Merge with the Infinite

"In the stillness of expanded consciousness, we transcend the boundaries of the self and merge with the infinite, discovering that the divine is not something we seek—it is something we are."

Transformation Beyond the Comfort Zone

"Transformation begins where the comfort zone ends—where consciousness reveals new possibilities beyond the confines of fear."

Unity Within the Tapestry of Existence

"Unity is not the absence of differences, but the recognition that every thread in the tapestry of existence belongs to the same sacred weave."

Unlocking the Infinite

"Consciousness is the key that unlocks the door to the infinite; it is not confined to the mind but reaches into realms unknown, where time and space dissolve."

Unveiling Time's Secrets

"Time, the great enigma, cloaks its secrets in moments—some lost, some cherished—challenging us to uncover the profound wisdom it quietly holds."

Unveiling the True Self

"To discover the self is not a quest to find something hidden, but a journey to remember who we truly are beneath the layers of expectation and doubt. In the quiet spaces of reflection, we uncover the essence of our being, and with it, the courage to live our purpose, unapologetically and with boundless authenticity."

Walking the Path of Inner Light

"When consciousness guides our path, every step becomes a reflection of our inner light and a testament to the infinite possibilities of purpose."

Whispers of Belief

"In the quiet chambers of the heart, belief whispers its powerful truths. Man is made by these whispers, for as he believes, he moulds his very essence and destiny."

Whispers of the Divine

Cosmic connection

"What you call coincidence, the soul knows as connection. The Divine weaves its will in the unseen—through people, moments, and the gentle pull of intuition."

- *Shree Shambav*

A Beacon of Light

"Even as the world shifts and time passes, the memory of you remains a steadfast beacon of light."

Awakening to the True Nature of Reality

"To awaken to consciousness is to see the world not as it appears, but as it truly is—a reflection of the infinite within."

Awe of Your Grandeur

"As the world celebrates your grandeur, we stand in awe of the profound beauty and love that you bestow upon us."

Between the Veil and the Tide

"We are forever standing at the shore of the unknown, the waves whispering truths too vast to hold."

Beyond Definitions

Dissolving the Self: "To know consciousness is to embark on a journey beyond definitions, where the boundaries of self dissolve into the oneness of existence."

Beyond the Illusion

"What you see with your eyes is a mirage; what you perceive with your heart is reality. The journey inward is the only path to truth."

Boundless Potential

"True freedom and happiness are not found in the absence of constraints but in our ability to rise above them. By letting go of the past with its heavy shadows and releasing our fears of the uncertain future, we discover the boundless potential of the present moment. Here, in the now, our souls find the space to truly soar, unencumbered by the chains of what was and what might be."

Cosmic Mirrors of Destiny

"Each Rashi is like a cosmic mirror, reflecting the energies of the universe onto the individual, shaping their soul's journey through time."

Depths of Transformation

"The most powerful transformations occur in the depths of our struggles, where we find the strength to rise, the courage to change, and the wisdom to grow."

Embracing Life

"Laughter is the soul's way of embracing life, turning trials into triumphs and mundane moments into cherished memories."

Embracing Life's Lessons

"Timeless wisdom does not seek to explain life, but to remind us that within every challenge, there is a lesson, within every hardship, there is strength, and that true growth comes from embracing the journey, not the destination."

Embracing the World Fully

"To awaken is not to escape the world but to embrace it fully, seeing the divine in all things."

Endless Blessings

"In the flow of life's streams and the embrace of night and day, your endless blessings soothe and uplift our souls."

Freedom Through Awareness

"Awareness is liberation. The moment you awaken to your true self, the chains of illusion fall away, and you walk free into the infinite."

Glimpsing the Infinite Cosmic Weave

"To touch the higher dimensions is to glimpse the infinite—to realise that life is a luminous thread in an eternal cosmic weave."

Guided by Faith

"When the heart and mind are united in unwavering faith, the vision of your desire becomes a beacon guiding you to your true potential. Constant contemplation transforms dreams into reality."

Harmonizing with Chaos

"Peace is not found in escaping chaos but in harmonizing with it."

Healing Through Inner Alignment

"Healing begins when we turn inward, aligning with the timeless wholeness of our consciousness, where balance is not sought but remembered."

Infinite Awareness in Stillness

"The stillness within is not the absence of motion but the presence of infinite awareness."

Keepsake of the Heart

"In the quiet sanctuary of my heart, your keepsake is a constant reminder of our eternal bond."

Lifting the Veil of Separation

"The illusion of separation is the ego's veil; when it lifts, we see the world not as fragmented but as a seamless tapestry of oneness."

Listening with Stillness

"Listen not just with your ears, but with the stillness of your being."

Living with Sacred Purpose

"To live with purpose is to align with the rhythm of the universe, transforming every moment into a sacred act of connection and meaning."

Love

The Infinite Language: "Love is the language of the infinite; it speaks not in words but in the silent embrace of unity."

Loving the Climb

"Growth is not in reaching the summit but in learning to love the climb."

Mosaic of the Soul

"Amidst the ebb and flow of life's journey, every experience, every tear, and every joy shapes our soul. Nothing is ever truly lost or wasted, as each fragment contributes to the mosaic of who we are."

Nourishing the Soul

The Seeds of True Happiness "True happiness blooms from within when we nourish our souls with gratitude, kindness, and the courage to let go of what no longer serves us."

On Spiritual Growth

"Spirituality is not a destination but a journey inward. It is in seeking, questioning, and understanding that we transcend the mundane, stepping into a realm where the soul's whispers guide us toward truth."

On the Role of Parents

"Parents are the roots that anchor us, the branches that lift us toward the sky. In their love, we find the strength to grow, the courage to dream, and the freedom to become who we are meant to be."

Purpose Beyond the Self

"Purpose is not something to be found; it is something to be lived. It emerges when the ego dissolves, and life becomes a joyful offering to the world."

Remembering Oneness

"To walk the spiritual path is not to seek the divine but to remember you have never been separate from it."

Remembering the Boundless Truth Within

"To awaken is not to seek something new, but to remember the boundless truth that has always been within."

Returning to the Essence

"The path beyond the self is not a departure, but a return—to the essence we have always been, united with the whole."

Sacred Act of Creation

"In the depths of our souls lie the seeds of infinite possibilities. Creation is the sacred act of bringing to light the timeless essence that resides within us, transforming the unseen into the seen."

Spiritual Pilgrimage

"The journey to self-discovery is a spiritual pilgrimage. Exploring our inner landscapes reveals the hidden treasures of our true essence."

Steps Toward the Sacred Dance

"Every moment lived in awareness is a step closer to the sacred dance where self and infinite become one."

Stillness Reveals Infinity

"To truly see the world, one must stand still; for it is in the stillness that the universe unfolds its profound simplicity and infinite wisdom."

The Bedrock of Existence

"Cast aside your fears of the unreal, for they are mere figments that vanish with the dawn. Cling to what is real and enduring, for it is the bedrock of existence, imperishable and everlasting."

The Blueprint of the Soul

"To understand your Rashi is to understand the blueprint of your soul—its strengths, its challenges, and the unique path it is destined to walk."

The Bridge to the Infinite

"Awareness is the bridge between the known and the infinite, where perception expands and the boundaries of reality dissolve."

The Courage to Shine

"It takes courage to let your inner light shine, for it reveals not only your strength but also your shadows. Yet, in this act, you illuminate the path for others."

The Dance of Truth

"Truth does not need to be sought; it reveals itself in stillness. When the mind is silent, the soul becomes the stage where truth performs its eternal dance."

The Divine Whisper

"Consciousness whispers softly in moments of stillness, guiding you toward a life of alignment and authenticity. To hear it, you must silence the world."

The Eternal Dance of Unity

"In shedding the layers of ego, we awaken to a reality where the boundaries of 'I' and 'you' vanish, revealing the eternal dance of unity."

The Eternal Dance of the Ocean

"You are not a drop in the ocean, nor the ocean in a drop—you are the dance of both, eternal and indivisible."

The Eternal Flame Within

"The light you seek outside is but a reflection of the eternal flame within. Turn inward, and you will discover that you have been the lantern all along."

The Eternal Light of Existence

"Consciousness is not a fragment of our being; it is the essence of existence itself—the eternal light through which we see, feel, and become."

The Evolution of Meaning

"Transformation is not a singular act but a journey through time, where the mundane evolves into the meaningful, and every thread finds its purpose."

The Fabric of Humanity

"Our humanity is woven into the fabric of our actions; with every step, we shape the world. Virtuous acts create pathways of light, while misguided ones cast shadows we must one day walk through."

The Flowing River of Knowledge

"A teacher is not a fountain of knowledge but a flowing river; the depth you draw depends on the thirst of your curiosity."

The Freedom in Uncertainty

"In the embrace of uncertainty lies the freedom to create anew."

The Gateway to Infinite Potential

"Consciousness is the gateway to all that is, and through it, we awaken to the infinite potential within."

The Gateway to the Infinite

"Consciousness is the doorway to the infinite, a silent bridge between the limits of the mind and the boundless expanse of existence."

The Gift of Stillness

"Stillness is not the absence of movement; it is the presence of awareness. In stillness, the universe unfolds its secrets."

The Gift of Transformation

"Embracing change is not simply about adapting to the unknown; it is about surrendering to the flow of life with an open heart, trusting that each transformation holds within it the seeds of new beginnings. In every shift, we find not only who we are becoming but also the courage to become more than we ever imagined."

The Illusion of Limits

"In the vastness of awareness, we discover that the limits we once believed in were only illusions veiling the infinite potential within."

The Infinite Horizon

"Your soul is the horizon where the finite meets the infinite. Do not confine it to the limits of your mind; let it expand into eternity."

The Infinite Journey of Transformation

"The infinite journey is not about reaching a destination but about embracing the transformation that unfolds with every purposeful step toward unity."

The Ink of Cosmic Intent

"Your Rashi, like the ink in a cosmic scroll, represents the commencement of your life's journey. It is a map, a mirror of the universe's intent woven into your being, that reveals the lessons you are supposed to learn and the growth you are destined to achieve."

The Intimate Journey Inward

"To explore the foundation of consciousness is to embark on the most intimate of journeys—a journey not outward but inward, where the infinite meets the core of our soul."

The Light of the Self

"When the sun sets and the fire dims, it is the light of the self that remains. It is the only guide that never falters, the only beacon that never fades."

The Measure of Love

"Time may measure life, but love gives it meaning."

The Mirror of Stillness

"In the still waters of silence, the true self is reflected. Only in quiet can you see who you truly are."

The Ocean Within the Drop

"Just as a drop of water holds the essence of the ocean, our consciousness contains the infinite essence of universal consciousness—interconnected, indivisible, and eternal."

The Paradox of Awakening

"To awaken to consciousness is to discover the paradox of being—an eternal dance between the seeker and the sought, where separation dissolves into unity."

The Path Within

"The journey inward is the longest and yet the closest path to the divine."

The Pathless Path

"The journey to your true self is a pathless path. There is no map, no destination—only the unfolding of who you already are."

The Polished Mirror of Truth

"The mirror of the soul reflects only when polished with truth and compassion."

The Power of Gentle Love

"In a world that often demands strength, it is kindness that holds the greatest power. It requires no grandeur, only the willingness to see others, to lift them with a gentle word or a tender gesture, reminding us that love, in its purest form, is a gift we can all give freely."

The Pulse of the Universe

"When we quiet the mind and listen to the whispers of the Divine, we feel the pulse of the universe within us, a reminder that our souls are forever intertwined with the cosmic dance of creation, forever part of something infinitely greater than ourselves."

The Radiance of Being

"Your being is not a flicker of light; it is the radiance of the infinite. To live authentically is to let this radiance shine unfiltered."

The Reflection of Actions

"Karma is not just a cosmic force—it is the mirror of our actions, reflecting back the fruits of our thoughts, words, and deeds. In the end, we harvest what we have sown."

The Resilient Spirit

"Strength is not found in never faltering, but in rising every time we fall, with renewed determination and resilience."

The Sacred Dance of Life and Afterlife

"In the embrace of the afterlife, we discover that life is a journey of beginnings, a sacred dance between the seen and the unseen."

The Sacred Dance of Unity

"When we awaken to the truth that we are not separate from the divine, we dissolve the boundaries of individuality and enter into the sacred dance of unity, where all of existence is one."

The Sacred Pause

"Silence in each inhale is a sacred pause, where the noise of the world fades and we reconnect with the serenity that resides in the heart."

The Sacred Truth of Oneness

"To journey beyond the self is to step into the sacred truth of oneness, where the illusions of separation dissolve in the embrace of infinite love."

The Secret of All Truths

"In the stillness of consciousness lies the secret to all truths, for it is both the seeker of the question and the source of the answer."

The Secrets of Stillness

"In every moment of stillness, the universe reveals its secrets to the patient heart."

The Silent Echo

"Silence is never empty; it carries the voices of everything unspoken, waiting to be heard."

The Silent Witness of the Stars

"The stars that form your Rashi bear silent witness to the unfolding of your karma. They do not define your fate, but rather light the routes available to you, allowing your decisions and actions to shape the trajectory of your soul's evolution."

The Song of the Departed

"No soul is ever lost, only carried by the wind, whispered through the stars, and written in the waves."

The Soul's Silent Secrets

"The universe whispers its secrets in the silence of your soul; to hear them, still the noise within."

The Soul's Ultimate Destination

"Unity is the ultimate destination of the soul's journey, where transformation bridges the finite and infinite, and purpose becomes the light that guides us home."

The Soul's Whisper

"Every silent breath is a whisper from the soul, guiding us gently toward the peace that awaits when we cease to seek and simply exist."

The Stillness in the Storm

"Consciousness is the stillness in the storm, the observer that witnesses all without judgment, revealing the infinite within the finite."

The Symphony of Existence

"Life is a symphony, and consciousness is the silent conductor. When you attune yourself to its rhythm, you become a harmonious note in the melody of existence."

The Thread Between Finite and Infinite

"Consciousness is the thread that weaves the finite into the infinite, a silent witness to both the vastness of existence and the intimacy of the self."

The Universe's Whisper

"Your zodiac sign is the universe's whisper, a celestial signature imprinted on the fabric of time. It reminds you that, while cosmic rhythms govern your existence, you have the freedom to dance in unison with the stars or carve your own path via the journey of free will."

The Unveiling of the Soul

"When the mind surrenders its illusions, the soul awakens to the truth: it was never lost, only veiled."

The Weight of Light

"Even the brightest light has known the burden of darkness, and still, it chooses to shine."

The Weight of the Eternal

"The truth is not heavy; it is the ego that adds the weight. When you let go, truth carries you effortlessly into the infinite."

The Whispering Spaces of Life

"The whispers of life are not found in grand echoes but in the quiet spaces—between breaths, beneath the fog, and within the folds of a simple story."

The Whispers of Our True Selves

"In the silence between our thoughts, we find the whispers of our true selves; it is there, amidst the stillness, that the heart speaks its deepest truths and reveals the path to our most authentic existence."

Timeless Wisdom's Call

"The wisdom of the ages is not merely a collection of thoughts from the past, but a living, breathing guide that whispers through the winds of time, offering timeless insights to those willing to listen, to grow, and to evolve with grace."

Transcending the Ego to Meet Ourselves

"To transcend the ego is not to lose oneself, but to awaken to a deeper truth—that in every other, we meet ourselves."

Uncovering Hidden Layers of Existence

"To journey through the dimensions of awareness is to uncover the hidden layers of existence, where every moment holds a universe waiting to be perceived."

Unveiling Sacred Layers of Existence

"Higher dimensions are not distant realms but sacred layers of existence, waiting to be unveiled through the stillness of awareness."

Whispers of the Divine

"In the silence between heartbeats, the whispers of the Divine call to us, reminding us that we are threads woven into the vast, eternal tapestry of the cosmos, connected by a love that transcends time and space."

Wisdom in the River's Current

"The river flows unceasingly, carrying wisdom within its currents; a true student learns not by waiting on its banks but by stepping in to gather what they seek."

Life Coach and Philanthropist

Shree Shambav is the visionary founder of the Shree Shambav Ayur Rakshita Foundation (www.shambav-ayurrakshita.org). He founded this institution with a lofty goal: to recognise human identity across gender, ethnicity, and nationality. Through this organisation, he wants to assist all communities in realising their full potential and the intrinsic beauty of life.

Shree Shambav, a Life Coach, is dedicated to supporting people on their journeys of self-discovery and empowerment. He assists people in discovering who they are, determining what inspires and drives them, and overcoming limiting ideas. His approach clarifies what one wants in life, assisting people through goal-setting and a step-by-step process for achieving them. He empowers people to make deliberate and responsible decisions, allowing them to identify their blind spots and evolve as individuals via the use of numerous strategies and tools.

The foundation's bold, uncompromising, and compassionate ventures are always aimed at initiating the "Inner Transformation" process. They focus on spiritual growth, personal growth, and self-healing while emphasising that true progress lies in "Inclusive Growth and Co-existence." This philosophy drives all their initiatives, encouraging a holistic approach to development and well-being.

Under Shree Shambav's leadership, the foundation has launched several impactful movements:

Shree Shambav Green Movement: This mission is to create a healthy, green, and clean earth through responsible water conservation and greening initiatives. The movement strives to make the world a green paradise by encouraging sustainable living and environmental responsibility.

Shree Shambav Vidya Vedhika (Vizhuthugal): This project aims to help students and children by offering training, books, stationery, and uniforms. It aims to provide the next generation with the tools and resources they need to excel both academically and personally.

Shree Shambav and his foundation exemplify the spirit of compassion, transformation, and inclusive growth via their work, which has a profound impact on individuals and communities around the world. His work exemplifies the power of acknowledging and nourishing the human spirit, creating a world in which everyone can reach their full potential and appreciate the beauty of life.

TESTIMONIALS

Journey of Soul - Karma - "We die in our twenties and are buried at eighty." Remember that nothing can stop someone who refuses to be stopped. "Most people do not fail; they simply give up." Shree Shambav deserves full credit. It allowed me to sit and consider what I might miss out on in life. The author has delved into every aspect of our daily lives. How can a seemingly insignificant change in these seemingly insignificant details bring us such joy? The Soul of Journey teaches you the "art of living" as well as the "art of dying."

Twenty + One Series - The rich cultural heritage offered a host in twenty + one short stories with incredible imagination, morals and values prevalent at a given time, influencing how people respond to a crisis or any situation. The author has recreated images with universal values and morals. The plentiful of fascinating from faraway lands would leave the modern play and story writers a cringe. The book supports trust and immeasurable values instilling hope for the new generations.

Death - "Shree Shambav's 'Death - Light of Life and the Shadow of Death' is an extraordinary masterpiece that delves deep into the profound questions surrounding our existence and mortality. The book's opening statement, 'Nothing ever truly dies; it simply ceases to exist in one form before resuming it in another,' sets the stage for a thought-provoking exploration of death's multifaceted nature. Shambav's remarkable ability to navigate the philosophical complexities of death and our universal fear of it is both enlightening and comforting. This book is a testament to the power of understanding and acceptance."

Whispers of Eternity - "Reading 'Whispers of Eternity' by Shree Shambav was a transformative experience that left me captivated from beginning to end. Each section of this exquisite collection delves into the myriad facets of existence, offering poignant reflections on life, death, and everything in between. Shree Shambav's verses are a testament to the beauty of language and the power of expression, inviting readers to embark on a journey of self-discovery and spiritual awakening. Whether celebrating life's simple joys or grappling with the complexities of human emotion, this book is a timeless companion that speaks to the heart and soul of every reader."

Life Changing Journey Series - "Life Changing Journey Series II Inspirational Quotes" is a remarkable collection that illuminates the path to self-discovery and personal growth. With its inspiring quotes and insightful reflections, this book serves as a beacon of light in a world often shrouded in darkness. Each quote offers wisdom, guidance, and encouragement, reminding readers of their inner strength and resilience. A must-read for anyone seeking inspiration and enlightenment.

Learn To Love Yourself – "A Heartfelt Guide to Authentic Self-Love." "Learn to Love Yourself" invites readers on a transformative journey to embrace their true essence in a world often focused on external validation. Through ten insightful chapters, it gently reveals principles of genuine self-love, guiding readers to deepen their connection with themselves. Beyond surface positivity, it encourages the cultivation of resilient self-acceptance, from embracing one's unique qualities to setting empowering boundaries. With inspiring stories and practical wisdom, this book is a trusted companion on the path to inner peace, fulfilment, and joy, helping readers build lives that reflect their authentic selves.

The Power of Letting Go – This book has been a gift to my spiritual journey. Shree Shambav's insights into attachment, personal growth cycles, and forgiveness are enlightening. The concept of seven-year cycles resonated with me, helping me understand the natural phases of life. I feel more empowered to let go of what no longer serves me and step into a life of freedom and fulfilment. A truly beautiful read!

A Journey of Lasting Peace – "A Journey of Lasting Peace" feels like a trusted friend guiding you through the maze of self-discovery. The 18 transformative principles are both practical and deeply resonant, addressing everything from gratitude practices to the art of letting go. Each chapter is infused with warmth and wisdom, making it easy to apply the concepts to my life. I particularly appreciated the emphasis on physical health's connection to mental well-being; it served as a wake-up call for me to prioritise my health. This book is an invaluable resource for anyone serious about personal growth!

Astrology Unveiled Series – "Profound, Logical, and Inspiring". What stands out in Astrology Unveiled is the author's dedication to making Vedic astrology logical and approachable. Each concept flows naturally into the next, backed by examples and exercises. The insights into karma and life cycles add a philosophical depth rarely seen in astrology books. Perfect for anyone seeking spiritual growth alongside astrological knowledge!

The Entitlement Trap - "Thought-Provoking and Challenging" The book challenges readers to confront their own sense of entitlement, and that's not easy—but it's essential. The Entitlement Trap doesn't offer a one-size-fits-all approach. Instead, it's a thoughtful, layered examination of how entitlement can limit our growth. The chapter on "Defining Your Own Hill" was particularly impactful, as it pushed me to reconsider which challenges are truly worth pursuing. A thought-provoking read for those willing to do the inner work to create a life they can be proud of.

Whispers of a Dying Soul – "A Soul-Stirring Reflection on Life's Unspoken Truths" **-** *Whispers of a Dying Soul: Unspoken Regrets and Unlived Dreams"* is a deeply moving exploration of the unexpressed emotions and unfulfilled aspirations that shape our lives in ways we often don't realise. This book invites readers to confront the powerful, often hidden impact of regret while guiding them through a journey of introspection and healing. Each page opens a space to reflect on the choices that define us—from moments of unspoken love to neglected passions—offering a gentle reminder to live authentically and courageously.

Whispers of the Soul: A Journey Through Haiku - is a mesmerising collection that speaks directly to the heart. Each haiku is a delicate brushstroke capturing life's fleeting beauty and timeless wisdom, inviting readers into moments of deep reflection and peace. This book is a balm for the soul, guiding us to find meaning in stillness and connection in simplicity. The themes of nature, love, and mindfulness echo universal truths, resonating with quiet, powerful grace. It's a book to be savoured slowly, cherished deeply, and returned to often. Truly, it is a gift for anyone seeking calm and clarity in life's chaos.

Whispers of Silence - Unlocking Inner Power through Stillness by Shree Shambav is a rare gem that beckons readers to pause, reflect, and reconnect with their inner selves. In a world that never stops talking, this book offers a profound exploration of silence—not as a void but as a rich and transformative space.

From the first page, Shree Shambav's writing resonates deeply, blending scientific insights with spiritual wisdom in a way that feels both universal and deeply personal. The author's ability to bridge the tangible and the transcendent makes this book an invaluable guide for anyone navigating the chaos of modern life.

The Power of Words: Transforming Speech, Transforming Lives - The Power of Words is a profound and enlightening guide that has transformed the way I approach communication. Shree Shambav masterfully uncovers the hidden influence of our words on relationships, self-perception, and overall well-being. This book doesn't just teach you how to speak; it inspires mindful communication that fosters connection and trust. The insights on replacing negative patterns like gossip and judgment with kindness and authenticity are truly life-changing. The practical strategies and engaging narratives make it an invaluable resource for personal and professional growth. A must-read for anyone striving to communicate with intention, clarity, and compassion. Highly recommended!

The Art of Intentional Living: Minimalism for a Life of Purpose - "The Art of Intentional Living is a refreshing guide to finding clarity in a cluttered world. With practical wisdom and profound insights, it inspires you to simplify, prioritise, and live with purpose. A must-read for anyone seeking balance and fulfilment."

ACKNOWLEDGEMENTS

To my grandfathers, grandmothers, mothers, fathers, aunts, uncles, neighbours, sisters, brothers, friends, and teachers they poured in endless moral stories, retellings of Ramayana, Mahabharata, Puranas, Upanishads, and so on.

My teachers, neighbours, and kindred souls. Who provided us with a stage to perform wonderful Puranic stories and were gracious enough to acknowledge our efforts.

The artists and translators of epics have served as a source of inspiration, invigorating our spirits, making these works accessible, and enabling us to grasp the profound depths and deeper dimensions they contain.

I also cherish the stimulating conversations I had with my wonderful mothers, Punitha Muniswamy and Uma Devi.

Our family's youngest member, Aadhya, who always overwhelmed me with questions, inspired this book.

I would likewise prefer to express gratitude to Mr Sivakumar, Mrs Roopa Sivakumar, Mr Akshaya

Rajesh, Ms Akshatha Rajesh, Ms Apeksha Prabhu, Mr Akanksh Prabhu, Mr Nikash Sarasambi, and Mrs Spoorthi Nikash for their valuable inputs.

I must thank Mr Rajesh, Mr Savan Prabhu, Mrs Revathi Rajesh, Mrs Rajani Sarasambi, and Mrs Manju Reshma, who encouraged me and often suggested writing a book. Their unwavering belief that I had something valuable to offer kept me going during my writing sessions.

Love you all,

Shree Shambav

www.shambav.org

shreeshambav@gmail.com

BOOKS BY – AUTHOR

Journey of Soul - KARMA

"Journey of Soul – Karma" is a heartfelt exploration of life's profound truths in our increasingly complex world. Addressing challenges, inequalities, and the quest for meaning, this book brings the timeless concept of Karma into focus. It emphasizes Karma not merely as philosophy, but as a guiding principle for our daily lives, inspiring us to walk a path of integrity and purpose. Through this journey, readers gain insights into how actions shape destinies, encouraging a life aligned with truth and compassion. It's a beacon for those seeking a deeper, more fulfilled existence.

Death - Light of Life and the Shadow of Death

In *Light of Life and the Shadow of Death*, the enigma of mortality is approached with clarity and compassion. Death is an inevitable certainty, yet it casts a lingering shadow of fear over our lives, stirring grief and despair as we strive to prolong our time on earth. This profound work examines the fate of departed souls and the heavy emotions we attach to loss. Yet, it offers a path toward accepting death and finding peace amid life's uncertainties. Exploring our origins, ethical values, and purpose, it unveils the sustaining truth of existence. The shadow of death, though daunting, is reframed as a shared, universal experience—one that calls us to confront our deepest fears with wisdom and grace.

Whispers of Eternity 150 Plus - A Symphony of Soulful Verses

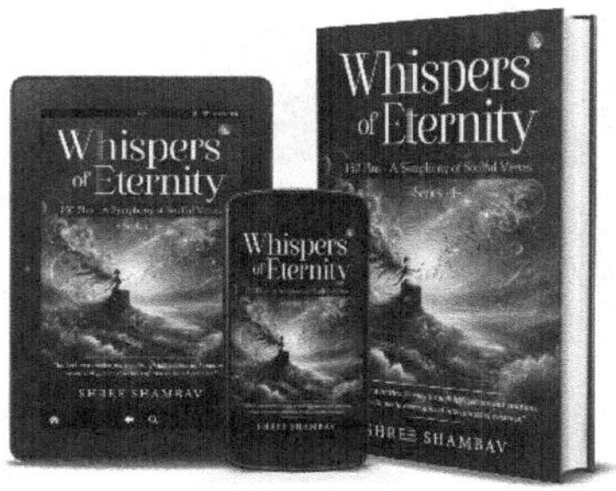

Step into the soul-stirring world of *Whispers of Eternity* by Shree Shambav, a collection of over 150 poems that capture the essence of the human experience. Divided into sections like "Through the Seasons," "Whispers of Hope," and "Threads of Unity," the book journeys through life's phases, emotions, and the universal connections that bind us all. Shree Shambav's verses touch upon nature, love, and spirituality, inspiring readers to find beauty in the everyday. Each poem is a finely crafted reflection, rich with insight and depth. *Whispers of Eternity* invites readers to pause, reflect, and embark on a timeless journey through the landscapes of the heart and soul.

Life Changing Journey Series I and II

In Life Changing Journey - 365 Inspirational Quotes Series I, Shree Shambav curates a powerful collection of 365 original quotes across fourteen chapters, each crafted to touch the heart of our daily lives. More than a simple compilation, this series speaks directly to personal experiences with wisdom and depth. Quotes like, "The most beautiful things are unseen but can be felt," echo the quiet beauty of life's intangible moments. Another, "Giving up is easier; holding oneself up is wiser," provides a guiding light in challenging times. Life Changing Journey reveals the transformative power of carefully chosen words, inspiring readers to find strength and new perspectives on their paths. Through Shree Shambav's work, readers are reminded of the wisdom and resilience hidden within each day.

Twenty + One - 21 Short Stories Series I and II

In *Twenty + One - Short Stories*, Shree Shambav brings to life the often-overlooked characters of nature—trees, animals, and mountains—revealing their intrinsic worth beyond mere utility. With poetic personification, he gives voice to these silent beings, some of whom are lucky enough to have names, titles, and rare human protection. Mountains, usually seen as mere landmarks, are depicted with reverence, emphasising their enduring presence. The stories build a bridge between humans and the natural world, showing that pain, grief, and resilience are shared across all forms of life. Shambav invites readers to empathise with the silent struggles of trees and animals, inspiring a fresh perspective on ecology and our responsibility towards the environment. This collection is a call to honour our connection to nature, encouraging readers to foster compassion and respect for all life.

Learn To Love Yourself

Learn to Love Yourself is a powerful invitation to turn inward in a world focused on external validation and superficial measures. Through ten transformative chapters, each offering a key rule for self-love, readers are guided to uncover their inner beauty, cultivate personal strength, and develop a solid foundation of self-acceptance. This journey goes beyond momentary happiness; it's about building an authentic relationship with yourself that fosters resilience, joy, and fulfilment. From embracing your unique qualities and practising compassion to setting boundaries and pursuing what makes you come alive, this book provides essential insights and practical guidance. Let *Learn to Love Yourself* be your trusted companion on this path, inspiring you to unlock the limitless potential within and find true inner peace.

The Power of Letting Go

The Power of Letting Go invites you to release attachments, fears, and expectations, guiding you toward true inner freedom and joy. With deep insights, practical exercises, and timeless wisdom, this book equips you to face life's challenges with resilience and grace. It explores the essence of attachment, embraces the power of seven-year growth cycles, and teaches the art of forgiveness as a key to a fulfilled life. Each chapter brings concepts to life through relatable analogies and real stories, making profound ideas both accessible and engaging. Let this book serve as your beacon for self-discovery and spiritual awakening, helping you navigate uncertainties and unlock your potential for a joyful, meaningful existence.

A Journey of Lasting Peace

A Journey of Lasting Peace is a transformative guide to self-love, inner peace, and personal strength, where Shree Shambav leads readers through 18 powerful principles for discovering their true selves. Each chapter explores vital themes, from the quest for inner peace and the importance of self-awareness to the healing practices of mindfulness and yoga. Through practical strategies, reflective exercises, and heartfelt stories, this book offers a clear roadmap to a more authentic and fulfilling life.

Whether you seek to embrace imperfection, establish healthy boundaries, or reconnect with nature, A Journey of Lasting Peace provides the wisdom to navigate life's challenges and find enduring tranquillity. Perfect for anyone on a journey of self-discovery, this inspiring work gently reminds us that lasting peace starts within.

Astrology Unveiled: Series I and V

Astrology Unveiled: Foundations of Ancient Wisdom invites you to unlock the mysteries of astrology, offering timeless knowledge rooted in the teachings of ancient sages. This comprehensive guide explores fundamental principles like Rashi, Graha, Bhava, and Divisional charts, making it an essential resource for beginners and intermediate students alike.

With logical explanations and practical applications, Shree Shambav skilfully blends ancient insights with modern understanding. Rich in examples, detailed explanations, and engaging exercises, this book serves as an illuminating path to mastering Vedic astrology.

Embark on a transformative cosmic journey, discovering how astrology can unveil your destiny, guide life's choices, and support your spiritual growth.

The Entitlement Trap: Get Over It, Get On It

Are you feeling stuck in a cycle of blame and dissatisfaction? The Entitlement Trap: Get Over It, Get On It offers a transformative path to reclaiming your personal power. This insightful guide helps you break free from the mindset of victimhood and empowers you to take control of your life. Inside, you'll discover how to redefine success, prioritize your true values, and live with purpose. Through practical strategies, you'll learn to embrace simplicity, connect with nature, and leave a lasting legacy. Get ready to shift from powerless to empowered and create a life you love!

Whispers of a Dying Soul: Unspoken Regrets and Unlived Dreams

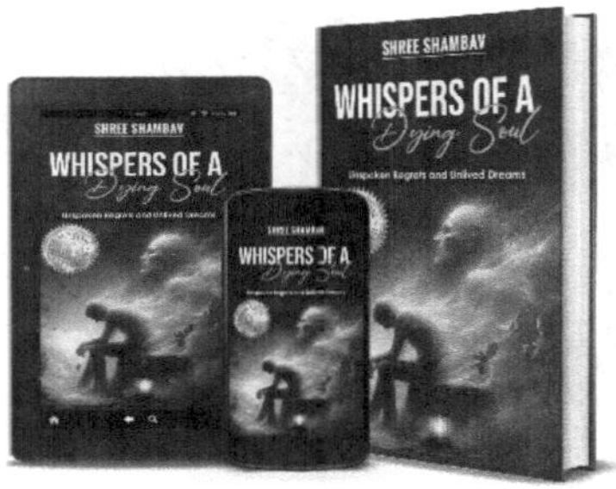

"Whispers of a Dying Soul", embarks on a profound journey that delves into the silent longings we often carry but seldom express. This powerful exploration uncovers the unspoken emotions that shape our lives—missed opportunities, unfulfilled dreams, and the quest for authenticity. Through heartfelt reflections and transformative insights, this book invites you to confront your regrets and turn them into powerful catalysts for growth and healing.

Whispers of the Soul: A Journey Through Haiku Series I to IV

"Whispers of the Soul: A Journey Through Haiku" is a poetic invitation to pause and rediscover life's hidden beauty. This transformative collection of haikus explores themes of nature, mindfulness, love, and the human journey, offering profound reflections on universal experiences. Divided into five series, the book delves into nature's elegance, the depths of inner stillness, the tenderness of human connection, the passage of life's seasons, and the mysteries beyond the self. Each haiku captures fleeting moments with timeless grace, guiding readers toward peace, self-discovery, and a renewed appreciation for life's simplest wonders. This is more than poetry—it's a soulful journey.

The Power of Words: Transforming Speech, Transforming Lives

The Power of Words: Transforming Speech, Transforming Lives illuminates the profound influence of our everyday language. This book explores how words can heal or harm, connect or divide, urging readers to embrace mindful communication. It delves into the "Sins of Speaking," such as gossip and judgment, while celebrating virtues like honesty, kindness, and authenticity. With practical strategies for transformation and a focus on the art of listening, Shree Shambav offers a roadmap to elevate our conversations. Perfect for both personal growth and professional development, this guide inspires readers to use their words to create peace, foster deeper connections, and lead a life of integrity and purpose.

The Art of Intentional Living: Minimalism for a Life of Purpose

In a world that celebrates more, The Art of Intentional Living invites you to embrace less. This powerful guide explores how minimalism can transform every aspect of your life—your space, your time, and your mind—by removing distractions and focusing on what truly matters.

Through simple yet profound principles, you'll learn to:

- Declutter your physical and digital space
- Prioritise what aligns with your values
- Create time for meaningful connections and experiences
- Cultivate a life of purpose, peace, and clarity

Awakening the Infinite: The Power of Consciousness in Transforming Life

In a fragmented world, Awakening the Infinite explores the power of consciousness to heal, transform, and unite. This book takes you on an experiential journey, revealing how awareness shapes reality and connects us to universal wisdom. Through spiritual teachings, introspection, and practical insights, it helps you uncover your soul's true purpose. With transformative practices, it guide you toward emotional healing, clarity, and personal growth. As you deepen your awareness, you'll forge a profound connection with yourself and the world around you. Embracing this journey leads to a life of mindfulness, authenticity, and purpose. Ultimately, it is an invitation to awaken the infinite potential within.

Beyond the Veil: A Journey Through Life After Death

Discover the Eternal Mystery of Life After Death What happens when we die? Is it the end, or a transition to something greater? In Beyond the Veil: A Journey Through Life After Death, explore humanity's greatest mystery through the lens of science, spirituality, and philosophy.

From near-death experiences to ancient spiritual teachings, this transformative book bridges the gap between the physical and the infinite, offering profound insights into the afterlife. Whether you're seeking comfort, answers, or inspiration, this journey will deepen your understanding of life, death, and what lies beyond.

Bonds Beyond Blood - Where love builds bridges, and bonds defy blood

Roots and Resilience is a poignant tale set against the quiet rhythm of suburban life, where a family grows strong through love, humility, and sacrifice. But when dreams collide with harsh realities and tragedy strikes, their foundation is shaken, and the true test of their bond begins. At the center stands a man, torn between honoring his past and forging a future amidst silent struggles within his marriage and the unspoken weight of grief. As the family navigates heartbreak, healing, and the quiet work of rebuilding, they discover that even broken roots can bloom again. This emotional journey is a testament to the resilience of the human spirit, the redemptive power of forgiveness, and the enduring strength found in choosing love—especially when life is at its most imperfect.

A Journey into Spiritual Maturity - 12 Golden Rules for Inner Transformation

In *A Journey into Spiritual Maturity: 12 Golden Rules for Inner Transformation*, Shree Shambav offers a soul-stirring path to self-discovery and inner peace. Blending timeless wisdom with practical tools, this book helps you release attachments, embrace change, and live with intention. Through inspiring stories and guided reflection, you'll learn to nurture self-love, deepen your relationships, and find freedom in authenticity.

Each golden rule is a beacon, illuminating the way toward a more meaningful, compassionate life. It is not just a guide—it's a companion for your soul's awakening. Let this journey lead you home to yourself.

9 789334 282184

Printed at Repro India Ltd.